MEET THE MYTHBUSTERS

Myths. Urban legends. Old wives' tales. Whatever their name, they share one thing in common. They all sound too good to be true. Handed down from one generation to the next, myths and old wives' tales have been around for a long time. Urban legends are more recent. These friend-of-a-friend stories are spread by word of mouth or over the Internet. Whether the information is true or not doesn't matter. Pretty soon everyone believes it—everyone that is, except Adam Savage and Jamie Hyneman, co-hosts of Discovery Channel's popular *MythBusters* show.

Adam   Jamie

Does a duck's quack echo? Can an octopus egg develop inside your stomach? Is it possible to drown in quicksand? When it comes to apocryphal stories such as these, the two intrepid trailblazers are determined to set the record straight. Using a combination of science and every trick in the book, they'll attempt to prove or bust the fifteen myths presented in this book—and with more than 30 years of experience in special effects and toy making between them, Adam and Jamie are more than qualified for the job!

Adam Savage started making toys when he was five years old. Since then, he has constructed everything from spaceships to bridges, from puppets to Buddhas, and, of course, toys. For the last nine years or so, Adam's work has included creating special effects for the film industry. He also teaches advanced model making at the San Francisco Academy of Art and has had his own sculptures showcased in art shows around the country.

Not only is Jamie Hyneman a whiz with parts and gadgets, he's also a wilderness survival expert, boat captain, diver, linguist, animal wrangler, machinist, and chef! A legend in the film industry, Jamie is the go-to man whenever an unusual prop needs to be fabricated, especially if it involves animatronics or robotics.

With the help of a crash-test dummy named Buster, Jamie and Adam will do more than explain how something may or may not be scientifically possible. Through trial and error, they will actually demonstrate it. So get ready to be dazzled by some pretty fancy wizardry!

CONTENTS

DOING THE EXPERIMENTS

Jamie and Adam use modern-day science to separate fact from fiction. But much of what they do on their show and in the pages of this book is dangerous! Under no circumstances should you ever try to copy any of their experiments yourself.

That doesn't mean you can't be a MythBuster-in-training! Throughout this book are experiments labeled "Do Try This at Home." Each experiment offers a safe and fun variation of the kind of science demonstrated in a featured episode by the MythBusters.

SAFE SCIENCE:

Before trying any experiment in this book, make sure you have an adult's permission. When an experiment involves cutting, hammering, or the handling of hot substances, ask for an adult's help. Clean up any spills right away, so that they don't cause accidents later.

LAB IN THE BOX:

You don't need a full-scale science laboratory or a closet full of expensive equipment to do the experiments. Just assemble a few basic items and store them in a simple cardboard box. Supplement these supplies with additional materials as necessary.

SUGGESTED SUPPLIES:

- Scissors
- Measuring spoons
- Measuring cups
- Plastic containers
- Ruler
- Measuring tape
- Masking tape
- Felt-tip pen
- Clock or stopwatch
- Straws
- Construction paper
- Cardboard
- String

BEING A SCIENTIST:

To obtain an accurate result, follow these foolproof steps when attempting an experiment.

- Before beginning an experiment, read the directions all the way through.
- Gather your materials.
- Decide what you think will happen in the experiment and write it down. That is your hypothesis.
- As you perform each step, jot down your observations. These notes are your data.
- When you have followed all the steps, write down the results. That is your conclusion.
- Compare your hypothesis with your conclusion. Is it different or is it the same?

Vroom, Vroom!

This schoolyard myth is almost as old as toy cars themselves. It claims that a toy car is faster going downhill than a real car. The MythBusters' build team has joined Adam and Jamie to put this myth to the test: Can a toy car beat a racecar using just the force of gravity? >>

MYTHBUSTERS™

DON'T TRY THIS AT HOME!

BY MARY PACKARD

JOSSEY-BASS
A Wiley Imprint
www.josseybass.com

Published by Jossey-Bass, A Wiley Imprint • 989 Market Street, San Francisco, CA 94103-1741

Developed by Nancy Hall, Inc.
Illustrations by Mike Altman

MythBusters: Don't Try This at Home! Book Development Team
Jane Root, General Manager, Discovery Channel
Gena McCarthy, Executive Producer, Discovery Channel
Sharon M. Bennett, Senior Vice President, Strategic Partnerships & Licensing
Michael Malone, Vice President, Domestic Licensing
Carol LeBlanc, Vice President, Marketing & Retail Development

Elizabeth Bakacs, Vice President, Creative Strategic Partnerships
Christine Alvarez, Director of Publishing
Elsa Abraham, Publishing Manager
Erica Rose, Publishing Associate

Jossey-Bass books and products are available through most bookstores. To contact Jossey-Bass directly call our Customer Care Department within the U.S. at 800-956-7739, outside the U.S. at 317-572-3986, or fax 317-572-4002.

Jossey-Bass also publishes its books in a variety of electronic formats. Some content that appears in print may not be available in electronic books.

Library of Congress Cataloging-in-Publication Data

Packard, Mary.
Mythbusters : don't try this at home! / by Mary Packard.— 1st ed.
    p. cm.
Includes bibliographical references and index.
ISBN 0-7879-8369-1 (pbk.)
1. Science—Experiments—Juvenile literature. I. Title.
Q164.P22 2006
507.8--dc22
                                2005030165

Printed in China
first edition

ON THE BELTWAY:

The first task is to find out how fast a toy car can go before the wheels break or wind resistance flips the car off its track. To test the wheels, the MythBusters build a mount that will hold the toy car on top of a modified belt sander. Adam runs the sander at top speed to test how fast the car can go before the wheels break. The toy tires pass the test with flying colors, but since the top speed of the belt sander is a wimpy 43 mph, it looks like the MythBusters will have to go to plan B.

Belt sander

WHEEL-Y FAST!

To reach higher speeds, the MythBusters substitute a real car tire for the belt sander. For safety's sake, the car is jammed against a building so it can't roll forward. A jack lifts the rear wheels off the ground so that they can spin freely. To make a smooth test track and to reduce friction, the team covers the treads, wrapping tape around one of the tires. Next, Jamie positions a mount on the tire that will hold the toy car in place. The engine is revved up. Wow! The toy car reaches 85 mph before flying off the mount. An inspection reveals that the tires remain in good condition. The tiny wheels can hold their own at speeds that a real car can achieve.

Here we go!

Real car tire

BUSTER SAYS:

Friction is an invisible force that appears whenever two objects rub against each other. It doesn't matter which direction something moves, friction pulls it the other way. Move something left, friction pulls it right. Move something up, friction pulls it down. This is true even of smooth objects. These objects might look smooth, but if you could examine them under a microscope, you'd see that they're actually rough and jagged. But don't knock friction. Without it, we wouldn't be able to walk, sit, or hold a pen. Everything would fall or slip from our grasp!

WIND FALL:

For the next experiment the build team makes a wind tunnel out of a leaf blower. After the toy cars are placed inside, a meter measures the speed at which the cars can stay suspended before flipping. It turns out that the maximum speed is between 73 and 76 mph. The wind tunnel experiment backs up the wheel-test results, suggesting toy cars can achieve speeds of more than 70 mph. The myth that a toy car can lick a real car is shaping up nicely—in the lab at least.

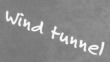

Wind tunnel

TOYING AROUND:

Each MythBuster designs a car to enter in the big race. Who can create the faster car, Adam or Jamie? Jamie takes his time experimenting with toy cars of different shapes and sizes. The van he tests is especially fast. When he turns it over, he notices that its wheels are positioned wider apart than those of the other cars. Jamie incorporates this into his prototype—the Silver Bullet— a sleek, aluminum car.

The wheels in the van are wider apart.

The Silver Bullet

May the best car win...

GETTING THE LEAD OUT:

Adam's opted for a chunkier model made out of lead. He's hoping that what his car lacks in design, it will make up in speed. The build team sets up a ramp in the shop for a preliminary competition. Sure enough, Adam's car is first over the line. Too bad it falls off the track! Ignoring his spill, Adam adds a few finishing touches and calls it a day.

BLAST FROM THE PAST

In the 1930s, a group of kids from Ohio started putting together their own "racecars." They built them from spare parts—discarded orange crates, old lumber, metal roller-skate wheels, and rope. When they were sure their cars were roadworthy, the kids raced them down some of the highest hills in town. One day, Myron Scott, a photographer for the *Dayton Daily News*, was almost run over by three kids speeding downhill on their engineless racecars. Luckily, Scott was able to dodge the speedsters and come up with a great idea, as well. He decided to hold the first official soapbox derby as a publicity stunt for his newspaper. That was in 1934. Since then, boys and girls all over the world have caught soapbox fever. To this day, gravity racing is a global phenomenon that can count among its competitors such luminaries as 1956 Heisman Trophy winner Paul Hornung, three-time NASCAR champion Cale Yarborough, and former *Tonight Show* host Johnny Carson.

ON TRACK:

After an exhaustive search for a straight but sloped one-quarter-mile stretch, the build team has come upon the perfect venue—Ski Boulevard in Lake Tahoe. Jamie and Adam go to work putting together the world's longest toy race track—1,320 feet of it! But most of their back-breaking effort is wasted. The super-long track is not practical. The hot sun causes the track to buckle, not allowing the toy cars to make it down without flipping over. The MythBusters know when they're licked! They shorten the track to 400 feet.

Jamie repairing the track

Dodge Viper

DOWNHILL RACERS:

With the shortened track, Adam and Jamie are ready to test run the toy cars. A white Camaro makes it down in 23 seconds. Then it's Adam's turn. His car is top-heavy and flips before it reaches the end of the track. Jamie's Silver Bullet, however, runs an impressive 18 seconds. For the final races, the Camaro and the Silver Bullet will race the real car, a Dodge Viper. Adam's car is scratched from the race.

CONCLUSION:

First up, it's the Camaro against the Viper, which is being steered by its owner. The Camaro leads for a short while, but the Viper easily crosses the finish line first. Now it's the Silver Bullet's chance to confirm or bust the toy car myth. After the signal blares, Jamie's car is the front-runner at 100 feet, but the Viper pulls ahead at the 200-foot mark for the win. The Silver Bullet clocks its best time, 17 seconds, but it's no match for the Viper. The Viper beats it by 4 seconds. It looks like this myth just got busted! Even though his car didn't achieve the overall best time, Jamie can't help but be proud of his car's performance.

BUSTED!

BUSTER SAYS:

The law of inertia states that objects at rest tend to stay at rest, and objects in motion tend to stay in motion. Imagine trying to get a huge circus elephant up from a sitting position. That's a lot of elephant to get moving. It would be easier to get a tiny mouse up and running. But once the elephant is running as fast as it can, it's awfully hard to stop it. The same is true for that big, heavy Viper and the toy car. The first 100 feet goes to the toy car, but once the Viper gets moving, it's really on a roll.

DO TRY THIS AT HOME

Perform your own road tests to find out how gravity, weight, and friction affect speed.

Materials:

- Several thick books
- 3-foot-long board
- Toy car
- Stopwatch
- Paper and pencil
- Tape
- 5 pennies
- Wax paper
- Sandpaper

1. Make a ramp by placing two books under the board. Roll the toy car down the ramp, timing it with a stopwatch. Record the time.
2. Add books to make the slope steeper. Roll the car down the ramp and record the time. Did increasing the ramp's angle cause the car to go faster or slower?
3. Put the ramp back to its original position. Tape five pennies to the top of the car. Roll the car down the ramp and record the time. Did adding weight to the car cause it to go slower or faster?
4. Remove the pennies from the car. Tape wax paper to the ramp, covering the top surface. Roll the car down the ramp and record the time.
5. Remove the wax paper and tape the sandpaper to the ramp, covering the top surface. Roll the car down the ramp and record the time. How did the speed of the car on the sandpaper compare to its speed on the wax paper?

BUSTER SAYS:

Increasing the angle of the ramp increases gravity's pull on the car, making it go faster. Extra weight also increases gravity's pull, and in the short run, increases the car's speed. The smooth surface of wax paper creates less friction on the car's wheels, so the car goes faster than when it rolls on wood. Sandpaper's rough surface increases friction and slows the car down.

BRAINBUSTERS

Are you an expert on what it takes to keep things moving? Take this true/false quiz and find out.

1. When two objects fall from the same height in a vacuum, the heavier of the two will reach the ground first.

2. If you drop a feather and marble from the roof of your house, they will both land at the same time.

3. Skiers put wax on their skis to keep them from going too fast.

4. Boots with grooves on the soles make it easier to walk on slippery surfaces.

5. The force that keeps objects from flying off into space is friction.

6. Wheels make it possible to move heavy loads more efficiently.

7. It's easier to stop a barrel full of monkeys than an empty barrel.

8. To make something start or stop, you have to overcome inertia.

9. When you throw a ball up in the air, the force that makes it fall is inertia.

10. A wave breaks on the shore because of gravity alone.

Answers on page 134

TALKING TO PLANTS

Pea Project:

Does talking to plants help them grow? To find out if this gardening myth is true, the MythBusters' build team came up with a plan to grow pea plants in seven separate greenhouses. The team would make sure that conditions in six of the greenhouses were the same except for one variable. In #7, the control greenhouse, the plants would be allowed to grow without being disturbed. After 60 days, the team would measure the results. **>>**

ADDED TWISTS:

The Mythbusters' build team gets to work building the greenhouses on top of Jamie's spacious roof. Four are set up to prove or bust the myth that plants respond to the human voice. Would kind words spoken softly influence their growth? Would screaming nasty insults cause them to shrivel and die? Two more greenhouses are set up to see if growing plants respond to music. One greenhouse will pipe in classical music; another will blast heavy metal. The control greenhouse plants will grow in silence. Once the greenhouses are up, the MythBusters' build team places ten pots with pea seeds in each one and sets up timers on a sprinkler system.

Grow, little seedlings, grow!

20th century composers etc

mental

STAY TUNED:

MythBusters' build team members each record messages to play to the growing plants, one nice and one nasty. A CD recording will be placed in the appropriate greenhouse, which will play nonstop throughout the experiment. Meanwhile, another team member selects music for his plants: soothing classical music for one greenhouse and rocking heavy metal for the other. The CD players are switched on and the experiment begins!

BLAST FROM THE PAST

In the 1960s, Cleve Backster, a lie detector expert, attached a polygraph to one of two houseplants in order to find out if plants have memory. Backster had a student yank up the other houseplant in the presence of the hooked-up plant. Later, he asked that student and five others to come into the room one by one and gaze at the remaining plant. In Peter Tompkins and Christopher Bird's bestselling book, *The Secret Life of Plants*, Backster reported that there was no reaction to the five innocent students, but that the meter went wild when the actual culprit showed up. Critics of the experiment noted the lack of adequate controls and concluded that similar results could have been caused by movement, static electricity, or fluctuations in temperature and humidity.

WAY TO GROW:

After a week, all seven greenhouses have sprouted seedlings. Some, however, have more than others. After four weeks, the plants are still growing well, but the peas growing in the two music greenhouses have the most seedlings. And the tallest, bushiest seedlings are rocking to the beat of heavy metal! The team decides things are going well and lets the automatic watering system babysit the plants.

A dying pea plant

PLAYING TAPS:

Yikes! Instead of the lush, green plants they left a month earlier, the MythBusters' build team returns to find drooping pea plants with yellow leaves. What went wrong? A quick check reveals a watering system malfunction due to a dead battery on one of the timers. The experiment is over, but since the plants in all the greenhouses were affected the same way, it is still valid.

HOW DOES IT WORK?

Plants are the only living things that manufacture their own food. They take in two ingredients—water and carbon dioxide, a gas that is found in the air. Energy from the sun turns these ingredients into food, much like an oven turns batter into cake. The whole process is called photosynthesis—*photo* for light and *synthesis*, which means putting things together. A greenhouse is the perfect place for photosynthesis to take place. It is covered from top to bottom with a transparent material such as glass or clear plastic to let the sun shine through. The greenhouse traps the sun's warmth, keeping it from escaping into the atmosphere. Add water, and plants in a greenhouse have everything they need to grow big and strong.

ENERGY ENERGY ENERGY ENERGY

CHLOROPHYLL

Carbon dioxide

Water

OXYGEN is RELEASED

GLUCOSE is formed

"PHOTOSYNTHESIS"

YOU REAP WHAT YOU SOW:

Adam and Jamie arrive just in time to help harvest the crop. To arrive at the final results the two MythBusters and the build team pull the plants out of the pots, rinse away the soil, count the number of pods, and weigh each plant.

Growing strong!

SILENCE IS NOT GOLDEN:

The results are in! The plants that were talked to grew stronger and heartier than the ones grown in the control greenhouse, although it didn't matter whether their words were friendly or mean, quiet or loud. And the plants that had music piped in grew best of all. But the plants with the largest bio mass and yielding the greatest number of peas were the ones grown in the greenhouse featuring heavy metal music.

Tasty!

CONCLUSION:

Jamie and Adam conclude that while the myth was definitely not busted, and their sample was too small to be confirmed, the results are plausible. Plants DO grow better when talked to, although what is said makes no difference. More interestingly, music helps more than talking, with the plants that grew in the heavy metal greenhouse of rock the clear winner!

PLAUSIBLE

BUSTER SAYS:

Stand next to a large speaker sometime and you'll feel the strong vibrations that loud music creates. Perhaps the strong vibrations from rock music affected the plants' growth. Perform your own experiment by playing the same rock music at different sound levels. Or try some loud classical music, like Tchaikovsky's *1812 Overture*.

DO TRY THIS AT HOME

See for yourself what plants need to survive.

Materials:

- 4 self-adhesive labels
- Felt-tipped marker
- 4 small clay pots
- Potting soil
- 4 small plants, such as geraniums or coleus plants
- Jar wide enough to cover one of the potted plants
- Soda lime (to be used by an adult only)
- Coffee scoop

1. Create the following labels: "No water," "No carbon dioxide," "No light," and "Control." Secure one label to each pot.
2. Fill the pots with soil. Plant one plant in each pot, making sure the roots are covered.
3. Place the "Control" potted plant in a well-lit spot, such as a windowsill, and water it regularly. This plant will get light, water, and carbon dioxide.
4. Place the "No water" potted plant in a well-lit spot, but do not water it.
5. Place the "No carbon dioxide" potted plant in a well-lit spot, too. Have an adult helper mix one scoop of soda lime into the soil. Because soda lime absorbs carbon dioxide it will keep the plant from getting its share, but it will not otherwise harm the plant. Water the plant and cover it with the jar. The jar will limit the plant's air supply and hold in all the water the plant needs for the duration of the experiment.
6. Water the "No light" potted plant and place it in a dark closet. Water whenever the soil is dry.
7. After two weeks, how do the plants look? Does one look healthier than the others? Which one?

BUSTER SAYS:

If the experiment was performed correctly, the plant marked "Control" should look the healthiest. That's because all its needs were met. It received energy from sunlight, water, and carbon dioxide and used them to make chlorophyll, a green pigment found in a plant's leaves. Chlorophyll is what converts these ingredients into food in the photosynthesis process. Because the other plants in the experiment were each deprived of a vital ingredient, they probably did not fare as well. If you continued depriving these plants, they would die.

BRAINBUSTERS

Do you have a green thumb? Take this true/false quiz and find out.

1. If you swallow a watermelon seed, a watermelon will grow in your stomach.
2. Sweet potatoes and yams are different names for the same thing.
3. The highly toxic poinsettia plant can kill a person or pet who eats its leaves.
4. Luak coffee is made from beans extracted from poop left by a luak, a small furry animal found in Indonesia.
5. Just a drop of poison from a castor bean plant can kill a person.
6. Without the nectar from the honeysuckle plant, humming bees lose their ability to hum.
7. The strong odor coming from an airplane's baggage area that caused a full-scale chemical alert and a 4-hour delay in the plane's departure was from a plant.
8. A horse could die from brushing against a certain strain of tree nettle plant.
9. Certain plants that grow in the rain forest can kill and digest small animals, such as frogs, birds, and rats.
10. The cotton grown within the cotton plant comes in one color—white.

Answers on pages 134–135

Round Trip:

Ever watch a goldfish in a bowl? Could anything be more boring than swimming in a continuous circle day after day? But what if the goldfish doesn't remember its route? What if every trip is a brand-new experience? Jamie and Adam will do their best to test the myth that a goldfish's memory lasts for only three seconds. >>

glub glub!

GOLDEN OPPORTUNITY:

The two MythBusters will administer a goldfish IQ test by each coming up with a simple maze for goldfish to navigate. Adam and Jamie will use the opportunity to compete to see which MythBuster is the better goldfish trainer. If they succeed, they'll prove that they're smarter than they think. And the goldfish will look pretty clever, too. Let the competition begin!

Do I have enough???

GONE FISHING:

Adam and Jamie shop for supplies—and fish—at a pet store. They buy two 38-gallon tanks, water filters, nets, ten goldfish, and enough fish food to feed a whale.

This is heavy!

BLAST FROM THE PAST

No one would argue that humans aren't intelligent. So what were college students in the 1930s thinking when they started swallowing live goldfish, creating a campus craze? It started at Boston College on March 3, 1939, when freshman Lothrop Withington, Jr. was running for class president. When a friend bet him that he wouldn't have the guts to swallow a goldfish, he decided not only would he do it, but he would use the opportunity to stage a campaign publicity stunt. On the day of the event, Withington invited the press, and as a large crowd gathered around him, he swallowed the wriggling fish in one gulp. Although Withington lost the election, he succeeded in starting a bizarre fad. On campuses all over the country, college students tried to see who could swallow the most fish in the least amount of time. The "fish wars" came to an end when the Boston Animal Rescue League declared the practice inhumane, and colleges outlawed the contest.

WET TEST:

The two set up their respective tanks, hooking up the filters and filling the tanks with water. In go the fish. Each MythBuster gets five goldfish to train. They have 44 days to train these fish to complete the maze. The fish seem to like their new homes. Now it's time to set up the mazes. Adam divides his tank into four sections, using clear plastic dividers that he makes himself. He cuts a hole in each one and drops fish food at one end of the tank. Will the fish swim through the holes to get the food? Stay tuned.

FISH TANK

FISH SCHOOL:

For his maze, Jamie uses bright orange openings that have mesh pockets into which fish food is placed. Jamie reasons that the fish will learn how to navigate the maze if he can get them to associate the bright orange with a food reward. In which tank will the fish learn better—in Adam's with its clear dividers or in Jamie's with its colorful ones?

TROUBLED WATERS:

The great goldfish challenge has been going on for a week. During this time, both Adam and Jamie have been working patiently with their fish, teaching them how to make their way through a maze. Then, on day 8, there's a problem with one of the tanks. The water in Adam's tank is cloudy. Adam investigates and discovers that one of his fish is dead. The most-likely cause is a filter malfunction. The filter isn't removing the ammonia created by fish waste. Perhaps the homemade dividers are interfering with the filtering system. It looks like Adam's challenge has shifted from training fish to keeping them alive! Adam drains the tank and fills it with fresh, clean water.

Please, not another one!

FIN-TASTIC:

Jamie's fish are healthy and apparently pretty smart, too. Jamie has succeeded in getting the fish to associate orange plastic with food. He has science on his side. Studies have shown that goldfish respond to color cues to earn food rewards. Jamie's next task is to get the fish to swim through the maze.

Orange = Food

How do I look?

How do I look?

TANK TIME:

Poor Adam! After six weeks, his experiment seems to be tanking! Two more fish have died, and he has just two students left. Nevertheless, he continues to work with his remaining fish. If one of his guys makes it through his maze first, he can still win the contest. Unfortunately, Adam's fish are not as motivated as he is. They make it through the first barrier, but then they backtrack.

HOW A-MAZE-ING!

No backtracking in Jamie's tank. The first fish makes it through the maze in one minute. Four others are right on its tail. Just one slacker lags behind. Perhaps coincidentally, this fish is the skinniest.

FIN POWER:

After 43 days of training, one of Jamie's fish holds the record at 25 seconds. Can the record be beat? Jamie's fish line up at the gate. Jamie replenishes the brightly colored mesh with food, and the fish are off. The first fish makes it through the maze in 40 seconds. The rest are on its tail. The original record still holds, but all in all Jamie's fish are the ones to beat.

LITTLE FLUNKIES:

Adam's fish are up next. It looks like they've been playing hooky. For whatever reason, they take between 3 to 20 minutes to find their food. Is it possible that their health suffered when the filter in their tank malfunctioned? Or would they have done better if the barriers in their tank were brightly colored like Jamie's were?

Oh, no!

CONCLUSION:

It's clear that Jamie's fish have learned how to navigate their maze to find food. From the improvement in their scores, it's just as clear that they've retained the information over time. Myth busted. George Barlow, a biology professor from the University of California at Berkeley, agrees that Jamie has blown away the myth that a goldfish has a three-second memory. The professor says, "Any task you can teach an animal and then retest later gives you a very objective way of evaluating whether it remembered it."

BUSTED!

DO TRY THIS AT HOME

Here are three simple IQ tests to try on your dog or on one belonging to a friend. Before you begin, make sure there is an adult helper with you at all times, and don't try this with any unfamiliar dogs.

Materials:

- 2 dog treats
- 1 coffee tin
- 1 blanket
- Watch or timer

Test # 1

1. Place a dog treat on the floor.
2. Cover the treat with the tin can. Make sure the dog sees you cover it.
3. Observe the dog's behavior.

Buster Says:
If the dog knocked over the tin to get at the treat, it's smarter than you think. This shows that it understands what scientists call object permanence—that objects exist even when they are out of sight. If the dog showed interest but was unable to figure out what to do, it is demonstrating that it is clever enough to know the treat is there. If the dog lost interest in the tin, it doesn't grasp that something can exist without being able to see it— a natural response for many dogs and babies younger than nine months old.

Test # 2

1. Throw a lightweight blanket over the dog's head and shoulders.
2. Time how long it takes the dog to get out from under it.

Buster Says:
If the dog frees himself within five seconds, it's a problem-solving genius. If it takes the dog a minute or longer, it's of average intelligence. If the dog shows no interest in freeing himself, its problem-solving skills are nonexistent. It's probably a good tail wagger, though.

Test # 3

1. Let the dog see you hide a dog treat under a chair or in a corner of a room.
2. Remove the dog from the room and play with it for a few minutes.
3. Take the dog back into the room.
4. Time how long it takes the dog to locate the treat.

Buster Says:

If the dog goes straight to the treat, it has a strong long-term memory. If it finds the treat within 45 seconds, its memory is above average. If the dog searches but does not find the treat, it has an average canine memory. If the dog shows no interest in finding the treat, it has probably forgotten that it's there. Don't worry if your dog scored below average on all of the tests. We love our pets not for how smart they are but because they give us so much love!

BRAINBUSTERS

Are you an expert on all things fishy? Take this true/false quiz and find out.

1. A goldfish has more chromosomes than you do.

2. In Medford, Oregon, a close friendship once formed between a carp and a pet parakeet.

3. Each year the mayor of a city in Belgium swallows a live goldfish.

4. Along with the National Marine Fisheries Service, Oregon State University has developed a school for salmon.

5. A parrot fish gets its name from its ability to repeat whatever is said to it.

6. A group of jellyfish is called a mob.

7. Male sand crabs are capable of changing their gender.

8. A certain species of starfish can recreate itself from a single severed piece.

9. A female blanket octopus is much smaller than the male of the species.

10. A phronima sedentaria shrimp lays its eggs in the hollowed-out body of a sea creature and swims away.

Answers on page 135

A Bellyful?

A woman was admitted to a hospital with stomach pains. When surgeons operated on her, they pulled a live octopus from her belly. How did it get there? Supposedly, while diving six months earlier, she had swallowed an octopus egg. The egg hatched and grew into a full-size octopus inside her stomach! Will this myth be busted or confirmed? Jamie and Adam are more than up for the challenge. >>

EGG-SPERT CARE:

At the Monterey Bay Aquarium in California, Adam and Jamie consult with Julia Mariattini, an expert in octopus behavior. Adam also has an encounter with a giant Pacific octopus. The multi-limbed creature from the deep just can't seem to keep its tentacles off the dashing Adam! At the aquarium, the MythBusters learn that octopus eggs are well tended by the mother, who blows jets of water over them to keep them aerated and regularly cleans them. So attentive is the mother octopus that she won't leave them to look for food.

Without her care, Adam and Jamie are convinced that it is impossible for an octopus egg to survive inside a human stomach.

SHOP TALK:

In order to determine if multicellular organisms can survive inside a human being, Adam and Jamie will create four artificial stomachs. First they make a trip to a lab supply store to buy four flasks, acid, salt, a voltage meter (for testing how much salt is in the water), and a thermometer. Last but not least, they purchase frog eggs and tadpoles from a frog farm in Florida. These tiny test subjects are small enough to be swallowed, common enough in nature for the myth to be plausible, and they don't need constant parental care.

I spy with my little eye...

TEST-TUBE TUMMIES:

Jamie and Adam fill the flasks with water and into each one place two tadpoles and two eggs. Now they'll tinker with the water to create four distinct environments inside their flasks. The first, the control flask, will represent the ideal environment for tadpoles to survive. The other three flasks will mimic conditions that are present in the human stomach. It won't be long before Adam and Jamie know which environment or environments allow these organisms to survive and which do not.

Piece of cake!

Tadpole

BLAST FROM THE PAST

So maybe an octopus egg can't survive inside a human, but what about other creatures that hatch from eggs? There are a number of myths dating from medieval times about people who have swallowed all kinds of eggs. Some were created to scare children into being good. In such a story, a child would typically swallow the egg of a lizard, toad, frog, or snake while playing in a garden. Soon after, the creature would hatch. If the child was lucky, he or she would throw up the newly hatched creature. If not, it would live inside its host, torturing the child with its evil presence.

FLASK #1:

A filter is added to the control flask. It will aerate the water, providing the ideal environment in which the eggs and tadpoles need to grow.

Aerator

FLASK #2:

The next flask is prepared by diluting hydrochloric acid and adding it to the water. The flask now has a pH level of 2, the same as stomach acid.

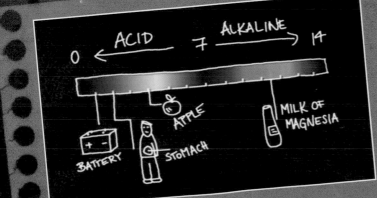

ACID 7 ALKALINE
0 → 14

APPLE
MILK OF MAGNESIA
BATTERY STOMACH

HOW DOES IT WORK?

For one of the flasks, Jamie and Adam diluted hydrochloric acid to mimic stomach acidity. The stomach secretes its own hydrochloric acid. A single drop of it can eat through wood. The pH scale runs from 0–14. Pure water is neutral with a pH of 7. Anything below 7 is acidic, and anything above is alkaline, the opposite of acidic.

FLASK #3:

The third flask is heated so that the water's temperature is 98.6 degrees Fahrenheit, the normal temperature of the human body.

FLASK #4:

The last flask has salt added to match the salinity found in a human gut. To find out what the salinity is, Adam uses the voltage meter to measure the electrical conductivity of his saliva. When salt is dissolved in water, the solution is a good conductor of electricity. The voltage meter measures how much electricity the salt water carries. Adam adds salt to the water in the flask until he gets the same conductivity that he found in his own saliva.

Is this necessary?

Tapeworms can make it through stomach acid.

HARD TO STOMACH:

To find out if there are any organisms that might survive inside a human, Jamie and Adam consult with James Mckerrow, professor of pathology at the University of California in San Francisco. The professor explains that stomach acid is designed to dissolve meat and other food. Instead of growing inside a body, an octopus or frog would end up digested. The eggs of certain creatures, however, such as tapeworms, have protection against stomach acid. Tapeworms, a parasite, have hard shells called cuticles. This surface armor allows them to make it through stomach acid to the intestines, where they gorge on as much food as they want. Before modern medical advances, it was not unusual for people to be infested with parasites. Sometimes, when the worms were passed, they would be bunched together in a wriggling mass. Seeing this, a person might easily imagine that they look like an octopus. Is this how the myth started?

DAY THREE:

As expected, the tadpoles in the flask containing the control group are thriving. The saltwater group is doing just as well. The tadpoles in the other two flasks died.

They'll never be frogs!

The saltwater tadpoles survive.

BUSTED!

CONCLUSION:

The temperature and acidity in the human body are too high for organisms other than parasites to survive. Myth busted.

DO TRY THIS AT HOME

Before it gets to your stomach, the food you eat begins to be digested by the saliva in your mouth. Here's an experiment that lets you observe how this first stage of digestion works.

Materials:

- 5 bowls
- 4 self-adhesive labels
- Pen
- 2 soda crackers
- Bottle of iodine with dropper
- Spoon
- Timer

1. Make four labels for four of the five bowls. They should read:

    Not chewed

    30 seconds

    5 minutes

    10 minutes

2. Place one soda cracker in the bowl labeled "Not chewed" and put one drop of iodine on it. What happens?

3. Chew the second cracker until it is very moist (about 20 seconds) and spit it into the unlabeled bowl.

4. Spoon one-third of the chewed cracker into each of the three remaining bowls. Wait 30 seconds. Then put one drop of iodine on the chewed cracker in the bowl labeled "30 seconds." What happens?

5. Wait five minutes and place one drop of iodine on the cracker in the "5 minutes" bowl. What happens?

6. Wait another five minutes and place a drop of iodine in the "10 minutes" bowl. What happens?

BUSTER SAYS:

A soda cracker is made up of starch. When iodine was dropped on the unchewed cracker, the cracker turned dark blue. This is the result of the chemical reaction that occurs when iodine mixes with a starch. When saliva was added to the mix, the chewed crackers turned lighter shades of blue. That's because saliva contains a special enzyme that helps break down starch into sugar. The longer the chewed crackers were left, the lighter the shade of blue. By the time iodine was added to the 10-minute bowl, there was no color at all. In 30 seconds, not much of the starch had been broken down yet. After ten minutes, the job was complete. Starch had been converted into sugar.

TRUE   FALSE

BRAINBUSTERS

Are you an expert on bacteria and digestion? Take this true/false quiz and find out.

1. Octopuses in captivity have opened jars of food with their tentacles.

2. In the 1700s, an Italian scientist concluded that food continues to be digested even after it has been regurgitated.

3. The acid inside your stomach is so powerful it can dissolve stainless steel.

4. There are more bacteria living inside your intestines than in any other place in your body.

5. Dog saliva is cleaner the human saliva.

6. Getting your tongue pierced can lead to heart problems.

7. People get hookworms by eating wormy apples.

8. Dogs are the primary carriers of pinworms.

9. Tapeworms are made up of segments, each of which can produce eggs.

10. Visitors at an interactive exhibit called *Grossology* can crawl through a 30-foot-long model of the digestive system.

Answers on pages 135–136

Deadly Daddies?

Are daddy longlegs the deadliest spiders alive? These common household spiders are rumored to have the most toxic venom of all the spiders. Supposedly, though, no one's ever been hurt by one because their fangs are not long enough to penetrate our skin. Why would nature provide a daddy longlegs spider with enough venom to kill an ox and fangs just large enough to kill a gnat? Sounds like a case for the MythBusters! >>

This is not fun!

MAJOR WEBSITE:

Before the daddy longlegs myth can be proven or busted, Jamie and Adam have to locate a bunch of them to use as specimens. Luckily, Jamie's garage turns out to be spider central. Jamie, a spider lover, is quite the hunter. Adam, though, is lagging behind. In spite of the fact that most spiders are harmless, Adam suffers from a mild case of arachnophobia, the fear of spiders. It's a good thing that Adam is brave enough to try to conquer his fear. He's determined not to let his arachnophobia keep him from doing his job. In the end, Adam and Jamie collect about 40 spiders.

WHO'S YOUR DADDY?

Daddy longlegs spiders are often confused with another group of animals that they greatly resemble. To make it more confusing, these creatures are also called daddy longlegs. Although they are member of the class *Arachnida*, they are not spiders. They have their own separate order, *Opiliones*. Unlike spiders, which have two body segments, opilionids have just one. They are also unable to produce silk to make webs.

Opiliones   Arachnida

THE PLAN:

To test the spider myth, Adam and Jamie will follow these steps:

- Extract venom from daddy longlegs spiders.
- Test the venom to see how toxic it is.
- Measure the spiders' fangs to find out if they're long enough to pierce skin.
- Test the venom on a human.

Milking a black widow spider for its venom

MILKMAN:

To help them with the first step, Adam and Jamie call on Chuck Kristensen, an arachnologist, a scientist who studies spiders. Kristensen also milks spiders for their venom. Chuck is so good at this skill he can milk 100 spiders per hour. Why does he do it? Research indicates that spider venom may one day be used in medicines that fight heart disease. Just one thimbleful fetches hundreds of dollars. Spiders are able to replenish their venom supplies, but the time this takes varies with the type of spider. Some components that make up the venom may be replaced very quickly, while others may take days or weeks to return after milking.

Carbon dioxide gas

WEB MASTER:

With Kristensen's expert guidance, the MythBusters will draw venom from the daddy longlegs. First, though, to keep the spiders from struggling and hurting themselves, Kristensen puts the spiders to sleep with a tiny amount of carbon dioxide gas. After they are milked, they will wake up none the worse for wear.

HOW SHOCKING!

The sleeping spider is carefully positioned with a special clasp beneath a microscope. To draw the venom out of the spider's tiny fang, Kristensen will use the longest, thinnest, hollow tube imaginable. First, he heats and stretches out the tiniest glass pipette until it is thin as a hair. The tube is positioned near the fangs. Then a tiny electric shock is delivered through the clamp, which causes the spider to produce venom. All that work yields just a few billionths of a liter of liquid.

BLAST FROM THE PAST

Just about everyone has heard the nursery rhyme "Little Miss Muffet." But did you known that the child in the nursery rhyme was based on a real little girl named Patience? While she may or may not have sat on a tuffet, it's very likely that Patience came into contact with lots of spiders. That's because her father, Dr. Thomas Muffet, was a 16th-century spider expert.

Why me?

OF MICE AND MEN:

Under strictly controlled conditions and with a veterinarian present, Kristensen compares the impact of daddy longlegs venom and black widow venom on mice. Should a mouse suffer any ill effects from the test at all, the vet will be ready to treat it with anti-venom medication. What are the results? The black widow venom is clearly more toxic than daddy longlegs venom. One part of the myth has been busted.

Black widow ←

THE REAL SKINNY:

The outer layer of human skin can be as thin as $\frac{1}{10}$ of a millimeter. Under a microscope, a daddy longlegs' fangs are measured at $\frac{1}{4}$ of a millimeter—more than long enough to break through human skin. That leaves just one more test. Is Adam up to the task?

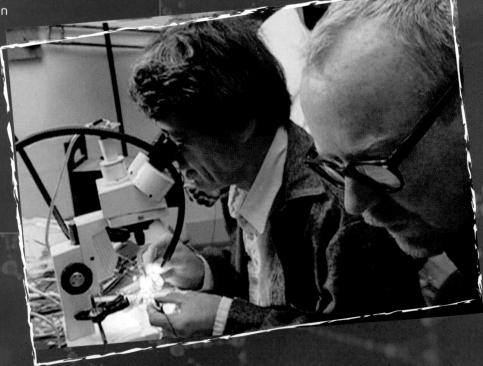

TUBE OF HORROR:

Poor Adam! He's about to live his biggest nightmare by plunging his arm into a tube full of daddy longlegs. The idea is to encourage the spiders to bite. So far, all the information indicates that he will be perfectly safe. But even with all the proper precautions taken, you should never do any testing on a human subject. As it turns out, since daddy longlegs are not the least bit aggressive, Adam has to sit there for quite a while with spiders crawling all over his arm. Finally, one bites him.

Never again!

CONCLUSION:

Adam feels just a teeny bit of burning, and the bite doesn't even leave a mark. The myth has been totally busted. Not only is daddy longlegs venom relatively weak, but these spiders are perfectly capable of biting when they feel like it.

BUSTED!

DO TRY THIS AT HOME

Only female spiders build webs. Here's how you can preserve one.

Materials:

- Spider web
- Hairspray
- Black spray paint
- White cardboard or poster paper
- Scissors

1. Find a spider web. Make sure that no spider is in it or waiting nearby.
2. Have an adult helper carefully spray the web with a light coating of hairspray.
3. Then have an adult helper give it a light coating of black spray paint.
4. Hold the cardboard behind the web so that it's just barely touching the web.
5. Cut the strands that are anchoring the web so it sticks to the cardboard.

BUSTER SAYS:

Spider silk is produced by glands in the spider's abdomen. Certain spiders lay down two types of silk, sticky and non-sticky. The first threads the spider shoots out are non-sticky and are used to hold the web in place. Then it shoots out more threads to create the web's pattern. These are the threads that trap insects. Depending on the spider, sometimes these threads are sticky, sometimes not. Why don't spiders get stuck in their own webs? Most bypass the sticky threads, using the non-sticky threads to navigate the web. Oil on their feet also helps prevent this from happening.

True   FALSE

BRAINBUSTERS

Are you a spider expert? Take this true/false quiz and find out.

Spiders!

1. Australian funnel web spiders are hard to milk.

2. Some spiders go fishing to find their food.

3. Spiders will never eat another spider.

4. The Brazilian wandering spider contains enough venom to kill 100 mice.

5. Spiders are named after a heroine in Greek mythology.

6. Spiders spin webs in random patterns.

7. Spiders chew prey well so it can be easily digested.

8. The female wolf spider abandons her babies as soon as they hatch.

9. All spider silk is used to make webs.

10. Bola spiders hunt for their food using a kind of lasso they make themselves.

Answers on page 136

TOOTHBRUSH SURPRISE

Hard to Swallow:

Is there more than toothpaste on your brush? The bristles of a damp toothbrush are an ideal place for bacteria to thrive. And when you flush the toilet, it's possible that germs from the bowl spray the area. The germs are fecal coliform, bacteria that are found in human waste. Might these tiny droplets land on your toothbrush? Hold on to your seat. Our brave MythBusters, Jamie and Adam, are about to flush out the truth. >>

CREATING A RACK-ET:

Adam constructs two toothbrush racks and installs them in the bathroom. The MythBusters need a broad test pattern, so they place 24 toothbrushes at different heights and distances from the toilet. Two additional toothbrushes are put in a glass on top of the toilet tank. Adam and Jamie will brush their teeth with these two brushes every morning.

This wasn't in my job description!

FLUSHED WITH SUCCESS:

The next order of business is to find out if toilets spray droplets of water. To this end, Jamie pours green food coloring into a toilet's tank, and Adam stretches a paper towel over the seat. One flush is all it takes. Sure enough, green specks of water stain the paper. One part of the myth has been confirmed. Now the MythBusters have to find out how far those tiny droplets can reach.

BLAST FROM THE PAST

Imagine living during a time when indoor plumbing didn't exist. Before the 1900s, most households in Europe and the United States did not have toilets. Country folk used outhouses, small outdoor structures with seats built over pits. City people kept chamber pots by their beds to use whenever the urge struck. Without sewers, they were emptied into ditches or right into the streets. No wonder cities smelled bad! One gentle breeze was enough to carry the nasty odors to other parts of the city. No one could escape the foul air, not even the royals. In the 19th century, while sailing along the Thames River on her yacht, Queen Victoria fainted from breathing the stench that filled the London air.

THE BIG BRUSH-OFF:

Before touching the toothbrushes, Jamie and Adam will wash their hands with antibacterial soap. Then they will rub each toothbrush with toothpaste, rinse it with a spray bottle of distilled water to prevent cross-contamination, and replace it in the rack.

Super-strength soap

KP DUTY:

Two additional toothbrushes will be kept in the kitchen to serve as the control group. Each morning, these toothbrushes will be rubbed with toothpaste, rinsed with distilled water, and put back into their holder. Their container will be completely covered by a glass dome, which, in theory, will keep them free of bacteria.

keep it clean

OPEN FOR BUSINESS:

As this routine is being followed, the toilet will be used for what it was designed for. A chart will track all bathroom activity.

BUSTER SAYS:

Fecal coliform bacteria are a group of bacteria that are passed through the fecal excrement of humans and other animals. They help in the digestion of food. *Escherichia coli*, aka *E. coli*, a subgroup of fecal coliform bacteria, can make people sick if ingested orally. *E. coli* have an amazing ability to grow at high temperatures. Under optimum conditions, they will thrive and multiply. Like most bacteria, *E. coli* grow best in dark, warm, moist environments with food. As they multiply, they form colonies that grow large enough to be seen.

POTTY MOUTHS:

At end of one month, all of the toothbrushes will be tested to find which have collected the most fecal coliform bacteria. Adam and Jamie are pretty certain that the toothbrushes closest to the toilet will contain the most germs. But that doesn't keep them from brushing.

These valiant seekers of knowledge will do anything in the name of science!

Here's another one.

CONCLUSION:

When the experiment is over, Adam and Jamie invite Dr. Joanne Engel, a microbiologist from UCSF, to visit their bathroom laboratory. Dr. Engel tests the toothbrushes for fecal coliform by rubbing each one on a petri dish smeared with agar, a growth medium. After incubating the samples overnight, Dr. Engel shows Jamie and Adam that all the dishes have sprouted pink dots. These dots are colonies of coliform bacteria, the family to which *E. coli* belongs. It made no difference how near or far the brushes were from the bathroom. Even the protected toothbrushes in the kitchen were contaminated! The unsettling fact is that fecal coliform bacteria are an unavoidable part of daily living. As Jamie remarked, "Poo is everywhere!" Adam and Jamie have learned a valuable lesson: Some myths are best left unanswered. Myth confirmed.

CONFIRMED

Fecal coliform bacteria—yuck!

DO TRY THIS AT HOME

In order to grow and multiply, bacteria need food. In this experiment, you'll see how one type of bacteria feeds on milk products and makes a tasty cultured cream. (Caution: Don't try this activity if you are allergic to milk products.)

Materials:

- 1 pint heavy cream
- Measuring cup and spoons
- 2 clean glass jars with screw-on lids
- Cultured buttermilk
- Sour cream

1. Equally divide the heavy cream into the two jars. Using clean spoons, stir 1 teaspoon buttermilk into one jar and 1 teaspoon sour cream into the other.
2. Taste each mixture with a separate, clean spoon. After using the spoons, do not put them back in the mixtures or you may contaminate the results.
3. Tightly screw the lids on the jars and store them in a warm place until the mixture is too thick to pour. This should take anywhere from 16 to 36 hours. Do not leave the mixture out for longer than this.
4. Taste the mixtures again. Which mixture is smoother? Which tastes more sour? Enjoy the cultured creams you have made on fruit or mixed with cereal. They will keep refrigerated for up to one week.

BUSTER SAYS:

The bacteria in the cultured creams you just made are called *lactobacilli*. These bacteria use the sugar found in milk products to multiply. As they feed on the sugar, each single-cell organism multiplies by dividing in half. In multiplying, the bacteria give off lactic acid, a waste product that gives the milk its sour taste and causes it to thicken. Different cultures give the milk products different flavors. The buttermilk culture has a milder taste and smoother consistency, while the sour cream culture tastes more sour.

BRAINBUSTERS

Are you an expert on toilets and toilet-related activities? Take this true/false quiz and find out.

1. A man named Thomas Crapper invented the toilet.

2. In ancient Greece, public restrooms were places where people often socialized.

3. While in space, astronauts use the same type of toilet that they use at home.

4. All bacteria are harmful.

5. A ski resort in Maine has found a new use for raw sewage.

6. A scientist in Japan invented a toilet seat that can analyze bodily waste.

7. Chamber pots used in Victorian times were ugly containers designed to be disposable.

8. A Chinese jewelry designer made a toilet out of gold.

9. The public restrooms in London are so old they're considered antique.

10. There is a 30-foot-tall tower of toilets in a museum in Wisconsin.

Answers on pages 136–137

Up, Up, and Away!

A popular myth tells of a small tyke who begins to cry while at a fair. To stop the wailing, the parent buys the child an enormous bunch of balloons. When the distracted parent looks away, she drifts up and off into the wild blue yonder. Could this really happen? And if so, how many party balloons would it take? The MythBusters' build team will spare no expense to find out. >>

> Let's get started...

HEADS UP:

For this experiment, the team will need one kid and a big bunch of balloons. But will the amount they need be too unwieldy to work with? The team members put their heads together. First, they find out how much weight ten party balloons can lift. According to their calculations, ten balloons should be able to lift 100 grams of paper clips. Converting from the metric system, they figure that it should take 46 balloons to lift 1 pound. They'll have to find one skinny kid!

> Yippee, I finally get to fly!

YOU'RE KID-DING!

They settle for a cute one. A member of the MythBusters' film crew has volunteered the services of his daughter. This brave four-year-old will be holding onto the biggest bunch of balloons she'll ever see. The team will need 2,070 balloons, and they figure they'll probably pop about 1,000 of them along the way. That's a lot of balloons! The MythBusters' build team is about to make some party-store owner's day!

BALLOONATIC:

The MythBusters are no strangers to unpowered flight. In a previous episode, Adam shot 3 miles into the sky. On that day, the MythBusters were testing whether it's possible to launch a man in a chair with helium-filled weather balloons. In 1982, Larry Walters bought 45 weather balloons, anchored them to the bumper of a jeep, and then strapped them to a sturdy lawn chair. After filling the weather balloons with several tanks of helium, he strapped himself in. With him was a pellet gun that he planned to use to deflate the balloons for a nice soft landing. But when he cut the chord, instead of lazily floating up among the clouds, he streaked into the sky to 11,000 feet as if he were shot from a cannon! Adam wasn't as adventurous. After rising 100 feet, he was ready to come down.

How do I get down?

Adam

BUSTER SAYS:

When weather balloons are inflated with helium, they measure 4 feet or more across. While that's much bigger than 11-inch party balloons, both types of balloon work pretty much the same way. Air is made up of different gases—oxygen, nitrogen, and carbon dioxide to name a few. Helium is a gas, too, but a molecule of helium weighs less than a molecule of any of the gases found in air. When you fill a balloon with helium, the balloon is less dense than the surrounding air. This causes it to float.

ALL TIED UP:

Could a bunch of party balloons really carry a kid away into the stratosphere? The MythBusters' build team is on the case. The three members go off to a party-supply store to buy cases of balloons and tanks of helium. While at the store, they get a free lesson in tying balloons. The secret to making really big bunches of balloons is to tie them into columns. Lots and lots of columns!

So, that's how it's done...

Only 1,798 more balloons to go!

HIGH TIMES:

The high ceiling in an abandoned airplane hangar makes the ideal place to test the balloon myth. The team decides to run a timed trial to see how long it will take to blow up 2,000 balloons. With three sets of hands and 26 balloons, they finish the job in two minutes, 20 seconds. Some quick math reveals that it should take just under four hours to pull off this caper. Time to start blowing more balloons!

FUN AND GAMES:

As the balloon tower gets taller, the fearless stunt kid is bubbling over with excitement. Some team members attach notes with the MythBusters' address to three balloons and let them fly off into the sky. She hopes whoever finds the messages will give the MythBusters a call.

Got your nose!

REALITY CHECK:

With half the balloons blown up, the team tests their progress with a sandbag stunt-double that weighs exactly the same as the stunt girl. They attach the balloons onto the sandbag double and let go. The dummy stays put. When they weigh the sandbag double while it's still attached to the balloons, they find that the 1,900 balloons they've already blown up cancel out just one-half of the little girl's weight. All their lofty calculations have been slapped down by gravity and helium lost from the balloons over time. Her magical mystery flight is starting to look like an impossible dream!

BLAST FROM THE PAST

In the early 1900s, the most popular lifting gas was hydrogen, a gas that's less dense than helium. When hydrogen mixes with air, however, it burns very easily. That didn't stop people from using this flammable gas to float dirigibles, huge airships that can carry passengers for hundreds of miles. On May 6, 1937, the *Hindenburg* airship was involved in a terrible accident. As it was landing, it struck an object. Hydrogen rushed out of the airship. A spark set it on fire, killing 36 of the passengers and crew.

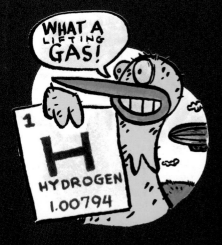

WHAT A LIFTING GAS!

1
H
HYDROGEN
1.00794

REAL DOWNER!

It looks like the MythBusters' build team will need twice the number of balloons than originally planned. Suddenly, everything is going wrong! Balloons are popping and flying up to the ceiling. Nerves are on edge. And with every minute that passes, the already-inflated balloons lose some of their helium.

I'm never going to fly.

FINGERS CROSSED:

The MythBusters' build team blow and tie, blow and tie, until they have 3,500 balloons tied into 250 columns. The little girl's moment is here at last. Strapped in and with safety lines in place, she is fastened to the columns of balloons. Will the balloons lift her? The team holds its breath and lets her go. Up she goes. Hurray!

CONCLUSION:

While it's possible to lift a child with party balloons, too many balloons are needed for the myth to be plausible. With the myth busted, one question remains: What ever happened to the message balloons? One balloon turned up at the Sequoia National Park, 300 miles away from the hangar. The whereabouts of the other two remain a mystery.

BUSTED!

DO TRY THIS AT HOME

Do some weightlifting of your own. You should be able to get your favorite action figure off the ground!

Materials:

- Box of paper clips
- Postage scale
- Pencil and paper
- 10 to 12 helium-filled party balloons, with strings
- Common household items, such as a pencil, a spoon, or a small plastic toy

1. Place one paper clip on the scale and record its weight.
2. Estimate how many paper clips you think one balloon can raise. Clip this number of paper clips together and attach them to a balloon.
3. Let go of the balloon. Does the balloon float? If it doesn't, take off some paper clips. If it floats too high, add some more paper clips until you are satisfied.
4. Multiply the number of paper clips on the balloon by the weight of one paper clip. You now know how much weight one balloon can lift.
5. Weigh another common household item, such as a pencil, a spoon, or a small toy. Based on your previous calculations, figure out how many balloons will be needed to lift the object.
6. Tie that number of balloons to the object. Did you achieve lift-off? Bravo!

BUSTER SAYS:

Weather balloons are really giant-size party balloons. Both are filled with helium, but while party balloons mainly function as decorations, weather balloons assist meteorologists in gathering important scientific data. Between 6 to 8 feet across in diameter, the balloons usually are equipped with radio transmitters, which send data back to the scientists. At the South Pole, these balloons are used to measure the amount of ozone in the atmosphere.

True   FALSE

BRAINBUSTERS

Are you an expert on balloons or just full of hot air? Take this true/false quiz and find out.

1. To steer a hot-air balloon shift your weight from side to side.

2. The *Hindenburg* was just 78 feet shorter than the ship *Titanic*.

3. The passengers on the *Hindenburg* had to settle for simple accommodations.

4. One of the passengers on the first hot-air balloon launch was a duck.

5. The first manned flight in a hot-air balloon lasted only 3 minutes before crashing.

6. Cold air takes up more space than the same volume of hot air.

7. The first attempt to cross the English Channel in a balloon was a success.

8. George Washington was present at the first hot-air balloon launch in North America.

9. The record for the highest solo hot-air balloon flight is 30,000 feet.

10. Hot-air ballooning has always been a very popular sport.

Answers on page 137

Answers on page 137

SINKING SHIP

Sailor's Warning:

There's an old sailor's myth that says that if you're on a ship when it's sinking, it'll suck you down with it. Jamie's impression is that if you are floating above a boat as it's sinking, it's not really going to pull you down. Adam is taking the wait-and-see approach. Both MythBusters are eager to get started testing this myth and finding out if it holds water. All aboard! **>>**

A hydrometer measures a liquid's density

TESTING 1...2...3:

One theory as to why this suction might occur is that air mixes with the water as it rushes up from the ship, creating a bubble effect. The bubbles make the water less dense and therefore cause people to sink. To test how bubbles affect floatation, Adam builds a 10-foot-high bubble maker out of PVC piping and drills it full of holes. They bring the rig to a local diving pool, along with a hydrometer, a floatation device that measures a liquid's density. The hydrometer will travel up and down depending on the amount of air in the water. Will water, made less dense by bubbles, be more apt to keep the hydrometer afloat? Or will the aerated water cause the hydrometer to sink faster?

WHAT HAPPENED?

As air is pumped into the water, the hydrometer sinks, proving that the bubbles made the water less dense. Time for Adam to put on his swimming trunks. Someone has to bring the hydrometer up from the bottom of the pool!

Come on in. The water's fine.

BLAST FROM THE PAST

In 1912, the ship *Titanic* sank on its maiden voyage. As it was going down, there were many firsthand accounts from passengers in lifeboats and rafts who claimed that their lives were saved because they had strong men rowing them far away from the suction of the sinking ship. Another account, however, contradicts this theory. Charles Joughin, the *Titanic*'s chief financial backer, found himself on the stern of the boat as its bow was sinking. He later said that it felt as if he were in an elevator going down. When he reached the water's surface, he stepped off the boat into the water, swam around for a while directly above where the ship went down, and eventually was picked up by a lifeboat. Which account is true? The MythBusters will do their best to find out

NOT SO SHIPSHAPE:

On to the next phase of testing. A second theory states that a ship sinking rapidly creates a vortex, or whirlpool, that sucks everything down with it. For the vortex theory, Adam and the hydrometer will serve as test equipment. A wooden box is attached to a cable to simulate the action of a sinking boat. The box is loaded with two 100-pound weights and the hydrometer is situated above it. When the box is dropped down the rig, the hydrometer sinks as well. Another 100 pounds of weights are added to the box. This time, the hydrometer sinks quickly all the way to the bottom.

One more curl...!

This is heavy!

Better him than me!

WHAT A DRAG!

Now it's Adam's turn. Adam sits on the weighted box. When dropped into the pool, it quickly fills with water—then sinks like a stone. As he goes down with the box, Adam feels himself being sucked into the vortex. The suction keeps him "glued" to the box. He sinks until the box hits the bottom of the pool—with a thud. Adam is a little sore but none the worse for wear!

Sinking fast...

BUBBLE TROUBLE:

Have you ever heard of the Bermuda Triangle—that treacherous place where many a ship has mysteriously disappeared? Modern-day scientists have puzzled over why these ships vanish without a trace. Perhaps a Greek mathematician had the answer all along. While sitting in his bathtub, Archimedes noticed that for something to float, the density of the liquid has to be greater than the density of the object. Fast-forward to the lab of present-day naval scientist Bruce Denardo. He is sinking balls in a beaker of water by forcing air bubbles in through its bottom. Apparently the airy water is not heavy enough to support the balls. Marine biologists know that there are large pockets of methane gas lurking beneath ocean beds. Changes in temperature can sometimes cause the gas to bubble up. Could air bubbles escaping from sea beds have caused the ships in the Bermuda Triangle to sink? Some scientists are beginning to think so.

CRUNCH TIME:

Does a sinking ship create a powerful drag on those in the water? After being sucked to the bottom of the pool, Adam is positive the myth will be confirmed. Jamie is not so sure. Testing with a real boat will resolve the myth once and for all. The search is on. The MythBusters need a good-size boat that will sink quickly. A wooden boat won't do, because they're too buoyant. It isn't long before the guys have located just the thing— a rusty steel boat that no one will mind sacrificing.

GOING UP:

Jamie and Adam don't know how many times they'll have to sink their boat before they get their answer. They need to be able to bring the boat back up to the surface after it's been sunk, so they devise a cable harness based on the boat's weight.

Jamie cuts holes.

GOOD TO GO:

They also cut holes in the boat that can be resealed. When the boat has to be retrieved, Jamie, in scuba gear, will dive underneath the boat to attach the cables. A quick name change to *Mythtanic*, and the boat is ready for launching.

MYTHTANIC

SINK OR SWIM?

At dawn, the *Mythtanic* is taken across the bay. It will sink under the shadow of a big crane that will hoist it up again, if needed. Adam volunteers to go down with the ship with a diving buddy. With 70 feet of water under the boat, this is a dangerous stunt. Unlike Jamie, Adam won't be wearing scuba equipment. So in case of emergency he has practiced learning to breathe through his dive buddy's regulator. A tugboat nudges the *Mythtanic* into position. The holes are unplugged, and the sea gushes in. The water is murky, cold, and deep.

Adam practicing breathing with his diving buddy

WHOOSH!

The boat is going down! But where is Adam? He was supposed to stay with the boat, but instead he bailed out early. The speed of descent caused him to panic and jump for safety reasons.

TAKE TWO:

Jamie dives underneath the boat and reattaches the cables lines. The boat is hauled up and the MythBusters try it again. This time Adam stays with the *Mythtanic*. The boat sinks, but Adam bobs on the water's surface, safe and sound.

Going...

Going...

Gone!

BUSTED!

CONCLUSION:

The myth is busted. No vortex was created when the 9-ton *Mythtanic* went down, proving without a shadow of a doubt that no vortex was created when the vastly larger *Titanic* met its end.

BUSTER SAYS:

If the myth is busted, then why did Adam sink to the bottom of the pool in the earlier test? The answer involves surface area. The large surface area of the *Mythtanic* allowed it to sink at a much slower rate than the compact 300-pound box. The speed of the box plummeting to the bottom of the pool created the vortex around it.

DO TRY THIS AT HOME

Why do some objects float and others sink? Try this experiment and find out.

Materials:
- Large plastic container
- Water
- Modeling clay
- Felt-tipped pen

1. Fill the container with water.
2. Form a small ball with some of the clay and drop the ball in the water.
3. Mark the water level on the container and remove the ball.
4. Form a larger ball with more of the clay and drop the ball in the water.
5. Mark the water level on the container and remove the ball.
6. Change the shape of the clay ball by creating a boat.
7. Place the boat on the water so that it floats.
8. Mark the water level with your pen.
9. Which object—the small ball, the large ball, or the boat—caused the water to rise highest?

BUSTER SAYS:

Whether an object sinks or floats has to do with its density. Objects that float, such as wood, are less dense, or lighter, than water. Objects that sink, such as stone, are more dense, or heavier, than water. So why did the clay both sink and float? Its shape changed. Water is displaced, or pushed out of the way, when an object is submerged. The amount of water displaced depends partly on the object's shape. The clay balls sank because they displaced their own volume of water. When the clay was made into a boat, though, its volume increased. The rising water level showed that a greater volume of water was displaced by the boat and the air it contains. This displaced water increased the water's upward thrust and the boat floated.

True   FALSE

BRAINBUSTERS

Are you a nautical expert? Take this true/false quiz and find out.

1. To create artificial reefs, retired New York City subway cars have been sunk off the coast of Delaware.

2. The wreck of the *Titanic* is continually being consumed by iron-eating swordfish.

3. It's impossible for life to exist near the hypothermal vents found in the deepest regions of the sea.

4. Considered the Mount Everest of scuba diving, the *Andrea Doria* is the deepest shipwreck ever to have been explored.

5. In 1986, a marine biologist found a skeleton with a perfectly preserved brain in the wreck of a sunken ship.

6. Though he was able to see the *Titanic*'s emergency flares from the deck of his nearby ship, a captain ignored them and went to sleep.

7. Unlike other shipwrecks found in other seas, those that have sunk in the Black Sea are completely free from rust.

8. Seaweed is a marine archaeologist's biggest obstacle when retrieving underwater objects.

9. The deepest areas of the ocean are called the pits.

10. Deep-sea divers wear special gear to protect them from toxic fish.

Answers on pages 137–138

RUNNING IN THE RAIN

Rain Check:

Most people pick up speed when they get caught in a rainstorm. That's because they think they'll stay drier that way. But is it true? Do you stay drier if you run in the rain? MythBusters Adam and Jamie have decided to put this myth to the test in their usual way. How? They'll use their way-cool high-tech tools and insatiable curiosity to create a scientific experiment on the subject. >>

THE SET-UP:

Jamie thinks it's common sense that the longer you're out in a rainstorm the wetter you'll get. His advice is to run in the rain if you don't want to get soaked. Adam has a different take. His theory is that although walking in the rain will keep you in the rain longer, only your head and shoulders will get wet. If you run, however, your entire front side will get drenched. To find out which MythBuster is right, the pair will create a rainstorm in a controlled environment. Then they'll walk through the rain in one set of coveralls, and run through it again in a second pair. After each run, they'll weigh their clothes. The wettest clothes will weigh the most.

A rare glimpse of Jamie WITHOUT his signature beret

DRY RUN:

Before they can begin their experiment, Jamie and Adam shop for latex body suits. They don't want perspiration mixing with the rain and possibly confusing the results. They also buy irrigation equipment that they'll use to rig up sprinklers. Last, but not least, they'll hunt for a suitable place to make it rain.

Been there—

—done that!

BEEN THERE, DONE THAT DEPARTMENT:

First, though, Adam and Jamie visit with Thomas Peterson and Trevor Wallis from the National Climatic Data Center. These two scientists once tested the rain/walk myth. After measuring out a 100-meter course, they waited for a rainy day. When it started to pour, one ran and the other one walked the course. Then they weighed their clothing. Their results showed that the runner was 40 percent less wet than the walker. Will the MythBusters' test confirm their findings?

HANGIN' IN:

Adam and Jamie have found just the right space to set up their indoor course—an airplane hangar at the Alameda Air Force base in California. The space is so perfect that Adam celebrates with an impromptu rain dance. The hangar's high ceilings make it ideal. In order for the homemade raindrops to behave as they do in an authentic downpour, they must fall from a height of at least 60 feet. That's the height they'll need to achieve terminal velocity, which occurs when the amount of air resistance equals the force of gravity's pull. Plus, the hangar is long enough to ensure an even spread of rain over a long distance.

Adam's impromptu rain dance

PIPE DREAM:

Jamie and Adam hang 150 feet of pipe from the hangar's ceiling and connect sprinkler heads to the pipes at 6-foot intervals.

RIDING HIGH:

To set up the rigging, they use a lift. Adam, never too busy to have a little fun, takes some time off from his work to ride around the hangar.

RAINMAKERS:

Now all the guys need is a water source. The Alameda fire department in California agrees to let the guys tap into a fire hydrant, as long as they get a meter to measure the amount of water they'll use. To get the water 60 feet above ground, they bring in a pump.

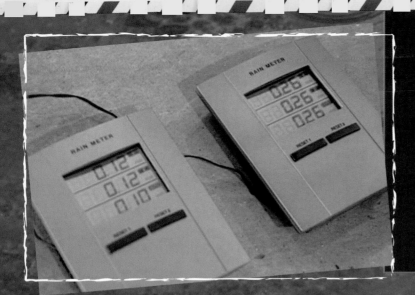

WAY-COOL TOOLS:

The course is set up to duplicate an average rainfall of between 2 and 3 inches per hour. Digital rain gauges will let the MythBusters know how many inches of rain per hour are falling. Adam figures the person who invented this gizmo didn't want to get wet while measuring rain!

FAN PLAN:

Jamie and Adam decide to add another element to their experiment—wind. They get some giant fans to create a driving rain, just like in a real storm.

Double Strength
Red Food Color
De Doble Fortaleza
Rojo Colorante
para Alimento

SEEING RED:

Adam adds food coloring to make the rain more visible. He uses a pipe to stir up some red rain in the holding tank.

BUSTER SAYS:

A rain cloud is made up of tiny water droplets. Water can take three different forms—solid (ice), liquid, or gas (water vapor). When weather forecasters talk about the amount of moisture in the air, they're referring to the amount of water vapor in the atmosphere. Heat from the sun causes water in oceans, rivers, and lakes to evaporate, turning into water vapor. Where does the water vapor go? It rises into the air and forms clouds. The drops fall to Earth as precipitation when they become too heavy to be held up by the pressure of air.

WET TEST:

The guys mark out a 100-foot-long course with tape. Then they don their cotton jumpsuits over their latex body suits. Each jumpsuit weighs 757 grams, or about $1\frac{1}{2}$ pounds, before getting wet. A high-speed camera records the MythBusters' movements, as well as every single droplet.

GAME PLAN:

Jamie and Adam each will go through the course four times: once walking, once running, once walking with wind fans, and once running with wind fans.

WEIGH TO GO:

After walking the course, both guys' coveralls weigh about 785 grams, which means they've soaked up 18 grams of water. Now for the run. The guys' coveralls are quite a bit heavier after the run, and weigh in about 798 grams. That's 14 grams more than the walking test. Windblown rain made the coveralls only a few grams heavier.

BLAST FROM THE PAST

Did you ever hear the expression, "It's raining cats and dogs?" While a downpour of cuddly pets have never been mentioned in meteorological records, there are many written accounts of rain delivering a lot more than raindrops. History is full of reports of fish falls, snake falls, and frog-filled rainstorms. A writer in ancient Greece once described what happened in Macedonia when a downpour of frogs pelted the city. So many of the little creatures fell on the streets that people couldn't help but step on them as they tried to make a quick getaway. More recently, people racing their yachts in the 1976 Olympics had the nasty experience of a maggot-filled rain falling on their heads. Though creature-filled rainstorms may sound like science fiction, there is a natural explanation for such phenomena. Tornadoes and waterspouts tend to suck up whatever is in their path—be it toads, snails, or jellyfish. As they lose strength, the twisters drop their cargo often hundreds of miles away. *Squish!*

CONCLUSION:

Myth busted! The overall results show that you absorb twice the rain per foot running than walking. It's better to walk in the rain than run—unless you like getting soaked, that is.

BUSTED!

DO TRY THIS AT HOME

How do water droplets form from vapor? To find out, make it "rain" in your kitchen.

Materials:

- Hot water
- Large glass jar
- Small plate
- Ice cubes

1. Pour hot tap water into the jar and cover with the plate.
2. Wait a few minutes.
3. Place the ice cubes on the plate.
4. What happens?

MEASURING A RAINDROP:

The next time it rains, measure the size of the raindrops that fall. As soon as the rain starts to fall, place a piece of heavy cardboard outside your window, then quickly bring it back inside. Use a ruler to measure the size of the drops. Raindrops can vary from about $\frac{1}{100}$ of an inch to $\frac{1}{4}$ of an inch across. Smaller drops usually come from light rain or drizzle, while huge drops fall from heavy downpours.

BUSTER SAYS:

The cold plate caused the moisture in the warm air to condense and form water droplets. This is what happens when warm, moist air meets colder temperatures in the atmosphere. Water vapor condenses, forming rain, sleet, hail, or snow.

True FALSE

BRAINBUSTERS

Are you an expert on the weather? Take this true/false quiz and find out.

1. Rainbows are most often seen on cloudy, rainy days.

2. Rain clouds are gray through and through.

3. One of the wettest places in the world is found in Hawaii.

4. Acid rain is caused by air pollution.

5. Water taken from certain wells in Australia is actually rainwater that fell about 6,000 years ago.

6. Cumulonimbus clouds can carry strong winds.

7. The tallest clouds in the sky are stratus clouds.

8. Seattle, Washington, holds the world's record for the most rain in one minute.

9. From the time water evaporates to the time it falls as rain, it will have traveled no more than 10 miles.

10. Most of the water droplets in a cloud end up as rain.

Answers on page 138

Quacking Up?

Have you ever read a list of odd facts posted on the Internet? Jamie and Adam have. One site they came across contained this intriguing piece of trivia: "A duck's quack does not echo." Of course, Adam and Jamie were not about to accept this myth without first doing a little research of their own. Step one? Find a couple of ducks. >>

DOWN ON THE FARM:

Jim Reichardt, whose family has been in the duck-farming business for years, has agreed to supply the MythBusters with two of his finest feathered specimens. Luckily, the ducks, Bob and Roy, don't seem to object to becoming test subjects for the planned experiment. They take to Adam and Jamie just like, well . . . ducks to water.

Bob and Roy, our test subjects

SOUND SCIENCE:

Roger Schwenkee is an acoustician, an expert in the science of sound. As the staff scientist at a company that manufactures top-of-the-line concert speakers, he's eager to help the MythBusters try to capture a duck's echo.

TAKING A SHOT:

Before involving the ducks, Roger conducts a preliminary test to make sure the equipment is working. Adam fires a starter pistol in an open field, and the shot is recorded on a tape recorder that is hooked up to a computer. The sound of the shot appears as a graph on the monitor. The initial shot shows up as a peak on the left of the screen, and the smaller peaks that follow it are echoes. It looks like all systems are go.

BUSTER SAYS:

We hear sounds because of vibrations in the air. When something vibrates, it moves the air around it. The moving air particles bump into neighboring air particles, causing them to vibrate and bump into the ones next to them. All these moving particles carry the vibrations through the air to your ear in what we call sound waves. The number of times a sound wave vibrates in a second is called its frequency. The sensations of these frequencies are known as pitch. A high pitch corresponds to a high frequency and a low pitch corresponds to a low frequency. Like light, sound can be reflected. If you shout in an empty tunnel, for instance, your voice will hit the tunnel walls and bounce back as an echo. You will get the best echoes off of smooth, hard surfaces.

DUCK TAPE:

It's time to get the ducks on tape. The first challenge is to attach a tiny microphone to Bob. The microphone acts as a trigger. Once Bob quacks, it will switch on the main mike a few yards away. That microphone will record the initial quack and any echoes that bounce back. The whole thing will be mapped out on a computer. On the screen, high-frequency waves appear compressed, while low-frequency waves are more stretched out. The biggest peaks represent the loudest sounds.

Microphone

Where's Roy?

FOUL MOOD:

Jamie is given the task of encouraging Bob to quack, but it looks like the cat has got his tongue. The guys decide to see if Roy is in a more talkative mood. Bingo! When Bob sees Roy, they both start quacking. It seems all Bob needed was someone who spoke his language. A duck quack is recorded, but there's no echo. Roger reminds Adam and Jamie that echoes are produced when sound waves hit something solid and bounce back. Since they've chosen an empty field for their test, there aren't many surfaces for the sound waves to bounce off, just grass and leaves. Roger thinks that if there were any echoes, the background noise probably drowned them out.

QUACKING FOR SCIENCE:

Adam and Jamie take their duck-quacking experiment to the lab. First they'll capture a crystal-clear quack with no echo. To do this, they place Bob and Roy into a special room that absorbs noise. The walls and ceiling of this anechoic chamber are covered with baffles, sound mufflers that are designed to trap echoes. Bob and Roy are quite chatty for this experiment and their quacks are recorded in record time. Adam and Jamie can't wait to see the results.

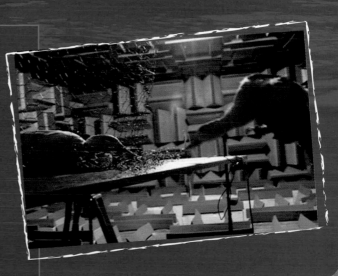

BLAST FROM THE PAST

Because the science of sound had not yet been explored, the ancient Greeks explained echoes the way they explained many marvels in nature—with a myth. In Greek mythology, Echo was a nymph, one of a group of woodland goddesses. Echo had one fault: she talked nonstop! But like all nymphs, she was playful and full of fun. To escape his responsibilities as supreme ruler of the gods, Zeus would often sneak down from the heavens to visit with the nymphs, even though his jealous wife, Hera, did not approve. One day, Hera followed Zeus to Earth, hoping to catch him with the nymphs. Echo tried to distract Hera by talking until Zeus could escape. Big mistake! When Hera found out what Echo had done, she punished her by taking away her power of speech. From that day on, all Echo could do was repeat the last word of the sentences of others.

A graph showing a quack recorded in the chamber

GOING QUACKERS!

Something fishy is going on! When Roger examines the results on the computer, the ducks' quacks look exactly the way echoes are supposed to look. The graph starts out with a tall peak followed by successively smaller and smaller ones. Since there can't be an echo in a room like this one, the fact that the recording of the quack has the same pattern as an echo is odd indeed.

GRAPHIC RESULTS:

Next, Roger brings Bob and Roy to a cavernous warehouse, the perfect site for echoes. Again the ducks' quacks are recorded. If there was an echo, it should appear on the computer screen, but nothing shows up. Roger has a hunch as to why this is so. If the echo sounds exactly like the quack, they might be hearing an echo but think they are hearing a quack. If that's true, all Roger has to do is tweak the results a bit. He filters out some of the extraneous quacks and enlarges the part of the graph where he thought the echo should be. Sure enough, it turns out the echo had been there all along.

Home sweet home!

CONCLUSION:

The MythBusters have proven that although a quack's echo might be tricky to hear, it does exist. Myth busted. And, in recognition to their contribution to science, Bob and Roy are rewarded with a comfy home by the Bay.

BUSTED!

DO TRY THIS AT HOME

See how sound bounces off different kinds of surfaces.

Materials:

- Several books of equal size and thickness
- Two cardboard paper towel tubes
- Watch that ticks
- Dinner plate
- Piece of cork
- Mirror
- Piece of foam
- Pillow
- Tin baking pan

1. Stack the books in two equal piles.
2. Place one tube on each of the piles.
3. Place the ticking watch in the end of one of the tubes. Listen for the tick at the other end of the tube. Can you hear it? Now listen at the end of the other tube. Can you still hear the watch?
4. Have someone hold a plate near the end of both tubes. Listen for the ticking again. Can you hear it?
5. Ask your helper to hold the piece of cork at the end of the tubes. Listen for the tick. Can you hear it?
6. Experiment with the mirror, foam, pillow, and baking pan in the same way. Which objects made the ticking sound louder? Which ones blocked out the sound?

BUSTER SAYS:

When sound waves are trapped in an enclosed area, such as a cardboard tube, they are amplified, or made louder. That's why when you placed the watch at one end of a tube and listened at the other end of it, the ticking sounded louder. In the experiment, when a hard surface such as a plate, a picture frame, or a mirror was held at the end of both tubes, the sound waves created by the ticking watch traveled through the first tube. After hitting the hard smooth surfaces, they bounced back and traveled through the other tube to your ear. The soft surfaces—the cork, foam, and pillow—absorbed the sound waves, so they could not bounce back.

True   FALSE

BRAINBUSTERS

Are you an acoustical expert? Take this true/false quiz and find out.

1. Sound travels more slowly through water than through air.

2. Sounds are louder in space.

3. Concert stages are designed to eliminate echoes.

4. A concert stage is often curved so that the audience can hear a performance equally well in any seat.

5. A hard surface reflects sound better than a soft one.

6. You hear thunder before you see lightning.

7. Marine biologists use sound to help them figure out water depth.

8. When you blow on a bottle of water, sound is produced because the water vibrates.

9. High-frequency sounds appear on a computer screen as waves that are far apart.

10. If you blow on two bottles, the one with more water inside will produce the higher sound.

Answers on pages 138–139

Star Struck:

According to legend, Wan Hu, a 16th-century Chinese astrologer of the Ming Dynasty, was determined to see the stars and planets up close. So eager was Wan Hu to visit space that he had a chair with 47 rockets attached to it specially built for him. After he climbed aboard, 47 assistants lit the rockets simultaneously. When the smoke cleared Wan Hu had disappeared. Did Wan Hu really make it into space? Jamie and Adam are on the case. >>

ROCKET SCIENCE:

Adam and Jamie will attempt to duplicate Wan Hu's launch down to the tiniest detail. Through their exhaustive research, they uncover the secret to making Chinese rockets. The first thing they need is bamboo, a tall grass that grows in Asia. Its hollow woody stems are used to make furniture, crafts, garden equipment, and—rockets. The MythBusters find just the size they need at a bamboo nursery in southern California.

Don't even THINK about trying this at home!

HOT STUFF:

Adam and Jamie are about to create some homemade fireworks—*something no one should try at home!* Using a traditional Chinese recipe, they cook up some experimental gunpowder. They mix the ingredients with roofing tar, which acts as a binder. Adam pours the stuff into the bamboo, tamps it down, and then wraps twine around it. This technique ensures uniform combustion, and allows the mixture to burn quickly but not explode.

GREAT BALLS OF FIRE!

When the rocket is ready, Jamie and Adam go outside for a test firing. A force gauge will measure the amount of thrust, the force needed to propel the rocket forward. They're hoping for 5 pounds of thrust. Because the fireworks should be powerful, Adam and Jamie take appropriate precautions by putting on ear protectors and clearing the area. Then they fire the rocket.

What happened?

FIZZLE FACTOR:

Blast-off is a letdown. The homemade rocket had only a half pound of thrust, too little to lift itself off the ground, let alone an astronaut! Adam goes back to his mixing bowl to see if he can produce a rocket with more power. Keeping the ingredients the same, he experiments with the ratio of the mixture. After several more test firings, Adam and Jamie concede defeat. They're not rocket scientists after all. It's time to get professional help from the experts.

BLAST FROM THE PAST

If Wan Hu wasn't the first person in space, then who was? That honor belongs to Yuri Gagarin, a Russian cosmonaut. On April 12, 1961, Gagarin orbited Earth aboard the spacecraft *Vostok 1*. The flight lasted 108 minutes. Instead of the landings we are familiar with today, upon reentry into Earth's atmosphere Gagarin ejected himself from the spacecraft and drifted down by parachute. The space mission was Gagarin's first and last.

LEAVE IT TO THE EXPERTS:

Eric Gates of Gates Brothers Rocketry and members of the Friends of Amateur Rocketry supply the MythBusters with the right mixture of gunpowder they'll need to get the rockets off the ground. Eric also suggests that Adam and Jamie conduct two launches. The first will be equipped with 47 bamboo rockets made according to the technology available in the 16th century. The second will have 47 modern rockets that pack a powerful 50-pound thrust. That way, the MythBusters can see what kind of launch Wan Hu could have gotten with modern equipment.

TIME OUT:

Now that they've got real rocket scientists on the case, Adam can use his considerable carpentry skills to build two replicas of Ming Dynasty thrones for the launches. Painted in red with decorative gold leaf, the thrones are designed for stability to give maximum liftoff. The MythBusters team contributes by baking tiles that look like Jamie and Adam. The thrones are truly awesome. Too bad they're going to be blown up!

Jamie!

Adam!

REALLY SPACEY:

It's time to head for the hills—well actually, the Mojave Desert in California. With a federal permit in hand, the MythBusters are cleared to put one of their most explosive myths to the test. Did Wan Hu win the space race before it had even begun? To find out, the amateur rocket scientists sift a large helping of super-strength gunpowder. To increase the pressure inside each rocket, Adam and Jamie have added a special nozzle to narrow the hole the exhaust will escape from. More pressure means more thrust and better performance—unless it all goes wrong. Time will tell!

Where's my stunt double?

COUNTDOWN TIME:

Buster the crash test dummy will be playing the part of Wan Hu. After Buster is strapped into the throne, no one sticks around to light the fuses. Instead they head to the safety of the bunkers. Once there, all the MythBusters have to do is flip a switch.

UP IN SMOKE:

10...9...8...7...6...5...4...3...2...1 Blast-off! Much like Wan Hu, Buster has vanished. But he's no astronaut. He's toast! Heat from the rockets caused multiple failures. The MythBusters find Buster not far from the launch pad. After they spray him with fire extinguishers, it's obvious that he's going to need a complete makeover. Buster is charred beyond recognition!

Bye bye, Buster!

Round two...

SEEING STARS!

Buster is dusted off and placed in throne #2. Will the best rockets that modern-day science has to offer send this now-crispy critter into space? The rockets should provide almost 2,500 pounds of thrust, more than enough power to send the 180-pound-test dummy into the wild blue yonder. After Jamie securely ties Buster to the throne, everyone again takes cover in the bunkers. The rockets go boom and Buster goes bust! The top heavy throne is briefly airborne before flipping over and skidding across the desert sand.

CONCLUSION:

Was it possible for Wan Hu in the 1500s to speed into orbit? Not!!! Yuri Gagarin's place in history is safe after all. Myth busted.

BUSTED!

DO TRY THIS AT HOME

Actually, don't try this one in your home. You might hurt someone or break something. Conduct this experiment outdoors.

Materials:

- 32-oz. empty plastic soda bottle
- cork
- 4 teaspoons baking soda
- ½ cup vinegar

1. Make sure that the bottle you use is clean and dry. Test that the cork fits snugly in the opening, but not so tightly that you can't pull it out.

2. Place the baking soda in the bottom of the soda bottle.

3. Pour the vinegar into the bottle and quickly cork it.

4. After shaking the bottle vigorously several times, aim the cork up and as far away as possible from yourself and other people.

5. Conduct this experiment outdoors, and wear safety glasses. Do not aim at anyone, particularly your little brother or sister.

BUSTER SAYS:

Chemical changes between the baking soda and the vinegar propelled the rocket you set off. When vinegar was added to the baking soda, a chemical reaction took place. The molecules of each ingredient broke down and recombined, producing a gas called carbon dioxide. The pressure of the gas expanding inside the bottle built up until it popped the cork with such force that the cork was sent flying. In much the same way, a rocket is propelled into the atmosphere by the blast of hot gases from its tail.

True FALSE

BRAINBUSTERS

Are you an expert on space travel? Take this true/false quiz and find out.

1. Lifting heavy equipment is easier in space than on Earth.

2. Each day several meteors make it into Earth's atmosphere.

3. On Earth, a star that has died would weigh more than an elephant.

4. One of the costliest parts of a shuttle flight is the landing because it uses up so much fuel.

5. An English scientist who lived in the 17th century discovered the laws of physics that govern modern-day space flight.

6. In 1963, Valentina Tereshkova became the first woman in space.

7. Before blasting off into space, Yuri Gagarin refused to eat breakfast for fear he'd get motion sickness.

8. The largest meteorite crater that has ever been discovered is one mile wide.

9. If you could weigh yourself on Pluto, you would weigh twice your weight on Earth.

10. Every second the sun gives off enough energy to supply the United States with power for one million years.

Answers on page 139

BREAKSTEP BRIDGE

All Fall Down:

The MythBusters are hot on the heels of yet another myth. Could soldiers marching in formation across a bridge have caused it to self-destruct? That's what happened on April 14, 1831, in Manchester, England. One theory states that the soldiers' marching may have matched the bridge's natural vibration. As the bridge absorbed energy from the marching men, the vibrations increased. Enough energy was added this way to bring down the bridge. Adam and Jamie are putting their heads—and feet—together in an effort to prove or bust this myth. **>>**

ALBERT BRIDGE
NOTICE

ALL TROOPS
MUST BREAK STEP
WHEN MARCHING
OVER THIS BRIDGE

Let's get started

LEFT, RIGHT; LEFT, RIGHT!

Adam is in charge of building a suspension bridge. Such a bridge has its roadway suspended from cables that are anchored at either end. Light and flexible, suspension bridges are capable of swinging in heavy winds—and to the marching of many pairs of feet?

MINI-MEN:

Jamie will create a miniature mechanical army to march on the bridge. Then the MythBusters will see if the rhythm of the soldiers' footsteps can make it vibrate. If it works, the vibrations should increase, much like bouncing on a trampoline causes a jumper to go higher and higher.

BUSTER SAYS:

All objects have their own natural frequency, the rate at which an object vibrates, or tends to swing. To find the natural frequency of a hanging object, just pull it to the side and release it. The object will swing back and forth at its natural frequency. Think of pushing someone on a swing. You time your pushes to the swing's natural frequency. If you didn't, it would be hard to keep the swing going. Resonance occurs when a series of small forces cause an object to build up a large amount of energy. So marching in step to a bridge's natural frequency can cause the bridge to absorb cumulative energy from the rhythmic footfalls. Some experts think that in extreme cases, these vibrations can be strong enough to cause a bridge's collapse.

TALL ORDER:

Adam's first-ever bridge will be 60 feet long and 6 feet high. He'll start by making 6-foot-long sections of road-deck that will be joined end to end. Then he'll build the uprights to support each end of the bridge. The goal is to tune the bridge to a vibration of about 3 hertz, the term for a unit of frequency. That's about three beats per second and about the same as a soldier's marching cadence. All that's left is to see if the bridge can be shaken to pieces by Jamie's soldiers.

Adam making the road-deck

Actuator

READY, SET, MARCH!

Jamie's on the hunt for a certain type of actuator, a mechanism that opens and closes valves. Jamie has a different use in mind, though. He sees its potential to make marching robots. He'll attach a crossbar to the actuator and insert a boot at each end. When the device is switched on, the boots will "march." Jamie places a green helmet on each device, and the soldiers are ready for duty. To power his miniature army, Jamie hooks up each robot to an air compressor.

SAG STORY:

Adam is positive his bridge was built to last. But for how long? Adam and Jamie are about to find out. Jamie places the marching robots on Adam's bridge and turns on the power. For the experiment to work, the boots have to hit the bridge with the same number of beats per second as the bridge's natural frequency. That should set the bridge in motion. Although the robots break the bridge, there's no evidence of harmonic vibration, just terminal sag. The bridge is just not strong enough to withstand the pounding of so many boots.

GOOD VIBRATIONS:

As Adam rebuilds his bridge, Jamie readjusts the speed of his robot army. But recalibrating so many marchers is proving to be time-consuming. So Jamie replaces the 12 mini-soldiers with one big one. This way, he can easily make adjustments to the robot's rhythm as he tries to match it to the bridge's frequency. Once the robot is turned on, the bridge vibrates a bit, a sign that the frequency is just about right.

Replacement soldier

FALL OUT:

The problem now, though, is that there's not enough weight to allow the vibrations to grow. The MythBusters have achieved a ripple when what they need is a tsunami. Jamie adds weight to the robot, but once again the bridge breaks. It's still not strong enough to support their experiment, and down it tumbles. Theoretically, a single footstep should start a wave by pushing the bridge down a little bit. As it comes up again, the next footstep will hit it and make it go down harder. If the timing is right, with each footstep, this wave will become amplified, becoming bigger and bigger. That's called matching the harmonic.

CAVING IN:

The guys give it one more try, but the project is proving to be too complicated and time-consuming. Once again the bridge fails before any real vibration gets going. One tantrum later, Adam decides to give up, and, for once, Jamie agrees.

Adam's tantrum!

BLAST FROM THE PAST

Nicknamed "Galloping Gertie," the Tacoma Narrows Bridge was not a bridge you'd like to drive across in high winds. This suspension bridge swayed both sideways and up and down, even in moderate winds. Attempts to stabilize the bridge were unsuccessful. On November 7, 1940, four months after its debut, the bridge went down. At the time, the wind speed measured a mere 42 mph. What had happened? Experts still aren't absolutely sure, but most agree that resonance was in some way responsible.

BUSTED!

CONCLUSION:

For this myth to hold water, the weight of the troop of soldiers would have to be very close to the maximum weight the bridge was designed to hold. On top of that, the frequency of the footsteps would have to match the frequency of the bridge perfectly. The odds of both things happening at the same time are slim to none. Adam and Jamie declare the myth busted.

DO TRY THIS AT HOME

Like a playground swing, a pendulum has its own natural frequency. The following experiment lets you see how a pendulum's length affects its frequency.

Materials:

- Ball of string
- Scissors
- Three heavy metal washers, all with the same weight

1. Tie a long piece of string to two stable objects, such as slatted chairs, to create a space about 3 feet long. Make sure the string is taut.

2. Cut additional string into three pieces, each a different length. Then securely tie a washer to the end of each length of string. You now have three pendulums of different lengths.

3. At evenly-spaced intervals, tie each pendulum to the line of string. Check to see that each pendulum can swing freely.

4. Swing each pendulum in turn and watch what happens.

5. Untie the pendulums. Cut the strings of two of them so that all three are of equal length. Reattach two to the line of string. Start one pendulum swinging and watch what happens to the other.

6. Attach the third pendulum to the string. Swing one pendulum and watch what happens to the other two.

BUSTER SAYS:

When suspended at different lengths, all three pendulums swing at different frequencies. Although each pendulum weighs the same, their varying lengths caused them to vibrate at different frequencies. The shortest pendulum had the highest frequency, which is why it moved faster than the other two. When the two pendulums were the same length, swinging one of them caused vibrations to be passed to the other through the string they were attached to. Since the second pendulum now shared the same natural frequency as its partner, it started to swing, too. That's an example of resonance. The same thing happened when you added the third pendulum. As long as they were all of equal length and weight, their shared frequencies allowed them to resonate and swing together.

BRAINBUSTERS

Are you an expert on sound and vibrations? Take this true/false quiz and find out.

1. A megabyte is a unit of frequency.

2. It's possible to break glass using just your voice.

3. An earthquake might cause one building to fall, but spare the one next to it.

4. Tap on two identical glasses filled with the same amount of water, and the sounds produced by each tap will sound different.

5. The lengths of a grandfather clock's hands help it keep the correct time.

6. When two swinging pendulums are of different lengths, the longer one will swing faster.

7. The collapse of a bridge during an earthquake is an example of natural frequency.

8. Tightening the string of a musical instrument will lower its pitch.

9. If you strike a bell that has been placed next to another bell of the same size and weight, the unstruck bell will also ring.

10. To swing higher, it doesn't matter how you time your pumps.

Answers on pages 139–140

Smoke and Mirrors:

Adam and Jamie are about to test one of the oldest myths they've ever come across. From the 3rd-century B.C., comes a strange tale of how Archimedes, a Greek mathematician and scientist, set fire to enemy ships using the sun's energy and mirrors. Adam and Jamie think that, given the right conditions, recreating this myth is a possibility. Besides, making a solar-powered weapon is right up their alley! **>>**

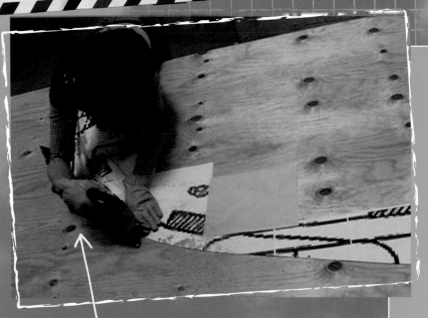

HOT TOPIC:

Historians speculate that Archimedes had soldiers use their bronze shields to create the mirrors he needed. So Adam and Jamie plan to use sheets of bronze to focus the sun's rays on a Roman warship. There's just one wrinkle in their plan. Roman warships, or triremes, no longer exist. Undeterred, Adam, Jamie, and the build team will try to construct a trireme of their own, using only materials available to the Romans in 215 B.C.

A team member constructing a Roman warship

Adam checks out the light meter and laser thermometer

SHOWING THEIR METAL:

Because bronze is so expensive, the MythBusters would like to find an alternative material. Armed with a light meter and a laser thermometer, the guys turn a spotlight on a range of materials—bronze; Mylar, a bronze-colored plastic; aluminum; and an ordinary household mirror. Bronze and aluminum reflect light best indoors. Adam experiments outdoors to see how all these materials reflect light from a greater distance.

ON THE BEAM:

When the eight-member crew aims the reflecting materials at the target, Adam discovers that it's not so easy to get them all focused at the same angle at the same time. How were 300 Greek soldiers with heavy shields able to manage such a feat? One thing is certain. Over a short distance, bronze works best, but for distances of more than 30 feet, glass reflects a more focused beam. Luckily, Adam's research reveals that the ancient Greeks would have had access to highly polished metal mirrors.

BLAST FROM THE PAST

Born in 287 B.C. in the Greek colony of Syracuse, Archimedes is considered to be among the most talented mathematicians of all time. While other children played, Archimedes was busy observing the world around him and thinking up mathematical equations to explain what he saw. His greatest contributions are in the field of geometry. Although Archimedes is known for inventing such useful things as his mechanical water pump, known as the Archimedes Screw, he spent much of his career designing and building sophisticated new weapons, such as catapults, pulley hoists, and levers that were used to destroy Roman ships. It was during the Second Punic War that Archimedes' invention is said to have been used. Bronze mirrors focused sunlight on Roman ships, setting them on fire. However, since written accounts of this achievement didn't appear until 800 years after the war ended, many people continue to debate whether the story is true.

Hemp

SHIPSHAPE:

Used by both Greeks and Romans, a trireme was a warship with three banks of oars. Adam and the crew are not going to build the whole vessel, just a section of the hull. They're not able to get the exact wood that the Romans would have used, so they're making do with spruce, a similar type of wood. Once the MythBusters have finished the construction, they'll caulk the vessel to make it watertight. Like Romans of long ago, they wedge hemp fiber between the planks and pour tar over the surface. Then they seal the raw wood with beeswax to protect it from the effects of saltwater. All these materials are highly flammable. It almost seems as if the Romans were trying to construct a warship that could easily catch fire!

Tar

GETTING FOCUSED:

The next step is for Adam to build the death ray. To do this, he has to figure out how many mirrors he'll need and how to arrange them to harness the sun's boat-burning potential. To arrive at the answer, Adam creates a miniature warship and 13 tiny warriors with mirrors that will (he hopes) focus the sun's rays into one lethal beam.

DISCO FEVER:

When the mirror-holding warriors don't work, Adam builds a miniature rig that looks a lot like a flattened disco ball. The rig holds the mirrors inside a common structure with a common focal point. As each mirror gets farther away from the center, its angle is increased so that it is still aiming at a common point.

HOT STUFF!

For the real death ray, Adam calculates that since the sun produces 100 watts of energy per square foot, 300 mirrors should produce 30 kilowatts of energy per square foot. Adam will screw 300 mirrors to a wooden frame measuring more than 400 hundred square feet. He and his crew have to drill 300 holes and then attach the mirrors at just the right angle for the maximum boat-burning potential—all before the sun reaches its hottest temperature of the day! It's a good thing Adam has the perfect tool to help with the job, a depth gauge that allows him to adjust each mirror's angle.

Depth gauge

ALL STEAMED UP:

At the Solar Two Project in California's Mojave Desert, solar power is tapped in a similar way. Almost 2,000 giant mirrors reflect sunlight onto a central tower containing molten salt, which is used to boil water. The steam powers a generator that makes enough electricity to power 10,000 homes.

BURNING QUESTION:

It's time to put the metal to the vessel. Adam has calculated that 60 feet is the hot zone, the spot where the rays will meet. So Adam's death ray is assembled 60 feet away from the warship. Then a fork lift raises the giant mirror. All systems are go. Will the ship go up in flames? The MythBusters are about to find out!

HEAT OF BATTLE:

As planned, the rays are focused on the ship. To take a temperature reading, Jamie puts on a fire suit and bravely wades up to the ship. The thermometer registers a measly 200 degrees Fahrenheit—about 350 degrees shy of ignition temperature! Even so, the wax on the ship is melting.

Jamie in his fire suit

GETTING HOTTER:

To boost the temperature, the crew holds up sheets of Mylar. The added rays bump up the temperature another 87 degrees. The tar begins to smolder but still no flames. Despite Adam's best efforts, the beams are not concentrated enough. Instead of meeting at a single point, the rays are scattered across the entire structure, diffusing the sun's energy. What a bummer!

Mylar

What a bummer!

CONCLUSION:

Adam and Jamie conclude that the beams from the mirrors just aren't concentrated enough. Because they're scattered across the front of the ship, the sun's energy is diffused. Besides, for this weapon to work, the enemy would have had to arrive at just the right time of day—when the sun is the hottest. Then they would had to have stayed perfectly still for the mirror to be aimed effectively. Considering how unlikely it is that these conditions would be met, Adam and Jamie agree that the myth is busted.

BUSTED!

In this experiment, you'll test how different surfaces reflect light.

Materials:

- Glue
- Matte (non-glossy) black construction paper
- 3 pieces of white cardboard
- Flashlight
- Mirror

1. Darken a room by drawing curtains or pulling down any shades that are there. Get an adult to help you if the windows are too high to reach safely. Another option is to conduct your experiment at night.

2. Lightly glue black construction paper to a piece of cardboard.

3. On a flat surface, prop up a piece of white cardboard and the mirror so that they are at an angle to each other.

4. Switch on the flashlight and turn off the lights. Aim the flashlight beam at the mirror so it reflects onto the white cardboard. Notice that the reflected light is almost as bright as the beam itself.

5. Replace the mirror with the other piece of white cardboard. Keep the flashlight aimed at the original piece of cardboard so that it reflects light onto the second piece. Is the reflected light as bright as when the beam reflected onto the mirror?

6. Replace the second piece of white cardboard with the black cardboard. Notice that the light is barely reflected at all.

BUSTER SAYS:

The best reflector of light is the mirror. That's because the surface of the mirror is flat and shiny, so almost all of the light bounces off it. When the mirror was replaced by the white cardboard, the reflected light was not quite as bright because the rough surface caused a diffused reflection, where light bounces off in many different directions. The black-covered cardboard reflected almost no light. The combination of the matte surface and dark color caused most of the light to be absorbed or diffused.

True   FALSE

BRAINBUSTERS

Are you a bright light? Take this true/false quiz and find out.

1. Light always travels at the same speed.

2. At night, a dark, rough surface is easier to see than a shiny, smooth one.

3. It is warmer in the summer because that is when the Earth is closest to the sun.

4. Staring at the sun too long can cause you to go blind.

5. A person can get sunburned through glass.

6. Concave mirrors (mirrors that curve inward) make objects look smaller than those reflected in a flat mirror.

7. Convex mirrors (mirrors that curve outwards) are attached to the outside of cars.

8. Amusement park funhouse mirrors are always flat.

9. Air can bend light.

10. Water can bend light.

Answers on page 140

BAGHDAD BATTERY

Turned On:

Everybody knows that electricity is a modern-day convenience. But is it really? The MythBuster build team is investigating an ancient myth that hinges on a single piece of evidence: a mysterious battery-like jar that dates back more than 2,000 years. Could it be true? Did ancient people really have electricity? **>>**

The original battery from Baghdad

GETTING A CHARGE:

Alessandro Volta, an Italian scientist, is credited with inventing the first battery in 1800. One hundred and forty years later, however, Wilhelm Konig, a German archeologist, noticed that an ancient earthenware jar could have been used as a primitive type of battery and published a paper on the topic. The jar, made somewhere between 250 B.C. to A.D. 250, is 6 inches high by 3 inches wide, about the size of a man's fist. Inside it were several items common to batteries: a copper pipe with an iron rod in its center and an acidic liquid residue. The jar was sealed with asphalt.

KEEPING CURRENT:

Because the original clay jar and others like it are in the National Museum of Iraq, the MythBusters' build team will have to create their own Baghdad battery. If it works, then they'll try to figure out what it was used for. The build team visits a pottery studio to try their hand at throwing pots.

POTTERY 101:

With the help of an expert potter, they bone up on their pottery-making skills. After practicing for a while, they get down to business. By day's end, they've made ten terra-cotta jars—each one 6 inches high with a ½-inch hole at the top.

A perfect jar!

BLAST FROM THE PAST

The Baghdad battery was found in the ruins of a village just outside the Iraqi city of Baghdad. This fertile region, which lies between the Tigris and Euphrates Rivers, was once called Mesopotamia, and is where ancient people settled to form the first city-state—an accomplishment that has prompted historians to refer to this region as the "cradle of civilization." The region's original settlers, Sumerians, have made many contributions to our modern society. They were the first to invent a writing system, and they are also responsible for coming up with the 12-month calendar, the water clock, indoor plumbing, the wheel, the plow, and the sailboat. Is it any wonder that batteries might have originated here as well?

BUSTER SAYS:

For electricity to flow continuously, it must run in an unbroken circle, or circuit. The circuit must be made of conductors, materials that carry electricity. Most metals make good conductors. To build his battery, Alessandro Volta used small sheets of copper and zinc and cloth spacers soaked in an acid solution. In the Baghdad battery, copper and iron were the conductors. An acidic liquid, such as lemon or grapefruit juice, would have permitted a flow of electrons from the copper tube to the iron rod. The electrical flow, or current, occurred when the two metals were connected.

Copper

Zinc

REALLY FRUITY!

It's time to turn the jars into batteries. The team experiments with different acidic solutions and metals. First, a strip of copper and a strip of zinc (the electrodes) are stuck into a lemon (the electrolyte). Wires from a voltmeter are then clipped to the metals. The acidic lemon strips electrons off the copper and allows them to flow to the zinc. The experiment creates an electric current of almost 1 volt.

Electrolyte

Voltmeter

HOW IRON-IC!

Because iron, not zinc, was used in the Baghdad battery, the team substitutes iron for the zinc in the next experiment. The iron-powered battery registered only a third of the volts. Some metals clearly conduct electricity better than others.

Next, vinegar and then grape juice are substituted for the lemon juice. In the end, the team chooses the lemon juice, the most powerful of all the electrolytes they tried.

Grape juice

Lemon juice

HEAD SCRATCHER!

The build team goes into mass construction mode. They create their version of the Baghdad battery by filling each terra-cotta jar with lemon juice. Then they encase ten iron rods with copper tubes. The rods are inserted inside the jars and the necks of the jars are sealed with tar. If all goes according to plan, the lemon juice will take electrodes from the copper and transfer them to the iron, creating an electric current. One jar registers .269 volts on the voltmeter. That's not a lot of power. But what if all ten jars were wired together? The results are better. The voltmeter shows 4.3 volts. A battery that's as big as a rack of bowling balls and as powerful as a half-dead flashlight might not pass a convenience test, but it is a battery, nonetheless. So what was this contraption used for 2,000 years ago? The build team is ready to find out.

Encasng the iron rod in copper.

Sealing it with tar

Final jars

Electroplating at work

WORTH ITS SALT?

One possibility is electroplating, which uses an electric current to coat a metal object with another metal. In this process, the object to be coated is suspended in a metallic salt solution (the electrolyte). Positively-charged metal particles drawn out of the salt solution are attracted to the negatively-charged object, which becomes plated with the metal. Artifacts from the same time period as the Baghdad battery have revealed that the ancients knew about electroplating, so it's plausible that this might be a use for the batteries. The build team uses the ancient batteries to provide the charge in their experiment. A negatively-charge copper medallion is immersed in a salt solution that contains zinc particles. Bubbles form on the copper, a sign that the experiment is working. When they come back the next day, the copper is plated with the zinc. The electroplating theory is definitely plausible. The team moves on to the second possible use for the batteries—pain relief.

BLAST FROM THE PAST

It's known that the Greeks and Romans used certain species of electric fish to relieve the pain of torn ligaments or gout. Patients would stand on a live electric eel until their aching limbs went numb. Could the Baghdad battery have had a less slimy, but similar, use?

STUCK-UP:

Acupuncture, the process of piercing the body with needles to relieve pain, has been around for more than 2,000 years. The build team pays a visit to a modern-day acupuncturist, one who is experienced in treating pain with needles and low-voltage electric currents. The doctor plies one member's arm with needles and hooks her up to the Baghdad battery. At first she feels a pleasing pulsing sensation. But when a needle heats up, the sensation becomes too intense, and the voltage is disconnected.

ouch!

PLAUSIBLE

CONCLUSION:

The medical experiment proved that the Baghdad battery might have been used to relieve pain. And the electroplating experiment was successful, as well. Myth plausible—on all counts!

DO TRY THIS AT HOME

Make a simple battery out of pennies and dimes.

Materials:

- Pencil
- Scissors
- Absorbent paper towels
- Tape
- 2 thin copper wires
- 15 silver dimes*
- Saucer
- 1 cup warm water with 2 teaspoons salt added
- 15 pennies

*After 1965, dimes were no longer made out of silver. If you can't find silver dimes, you can substitute coin-shaped circles of aluminum foil.

1. Draw and cut out 15 coin-sized circles from the paper towels.
2. Tape one copper wire to a dime and put it in the saucer. Dip a paper circle in the salty water and place it on top of the dime. Place a penny on top of that.
3. Continue stacking in this order until you've used all the coins and all the paper circles. The stack should end with a penny. Tape the other piece of wire to the penny.
4. Take the ends of both wires and touch the tips to your tongue. What do you feel? (Caution: Never try this with a real battery!)

BUSTER SAYS:

You should have felt a slight tingling in your tongue. The silver, copper, and saltwater produced an electric current that caused the tingling. That current was weak, but if you were to stack more coins and paper circles, your battery would be bigger and so would the current it produced.

TRUE   FALSE

BRAINBUSTERS

Are you an electrical whiz? Take this true/false quiz and find out.

1. In the previous experiment, the penny is the electrolyte.

2. Static electricity can cause your hair to stand on end.

3. Lightning is the same kind of spark that happens when you walk across a carpeted floor and touch a metal doorknob.

4. Electricity can make dead muscles twitch as though they are alive.

5. All batteries "die" because they get rusty inside.

6. Electroplating is used in the manufacture of automobiles.

7. An electron makes up the central part of atom.

8. An electric current is actually electrolytes pouring through wire.

9. Nails and screws are coated with plastic to keep them from rusting.

10. The process of rust-proofing is called edisonation, after its inventor, Thomas Edison.

Answers on pages 140–141

Sink or Swim?

Is quicksand the fearsome force of nature you've always heard about? It is, if you believe what you've seen on TV and in the movies. But the MythBusters are not so sure. To find out, Adam and Jamie will try to create killer quicksand on their own. First, though, they'll need a mighty big container and a whole lot of sand. **>>**

That was really satisfying.

TANKS A LOT!
Luckily the MythBusters have just the thing: a 2,000-gallon-tank that they used in an earlier experiment. With his trusty reciprocating saw, Adam slices off the tank's top, turning it into an eight-foot-tall sandbox.

A HOLE LOT OF FUN:
Adam drills holes in the tank and then covers them with gauze, a porous fabric that will allow water to escape from the tank but keep the sand in. Meanwhile, Jamie and his team work on the diffuser, which is nothing more than a flat piece of wood with holes punched through it. Jamie and Adam cover these holes with gauze as well. The diffuser will sit at the bottom of the tank on top of an irrigation pump. Once the tank has been filled with sand, the MythBusters will pump water up through the diffuser. That way, water can be pumped through the holes, but the sand can't flow back into the pump.

HOLLYWOOD HYPE:

Back in the 1930s and '40s, Johnny Weissmuller played Tarzan the Ape Man on the big screen. Moviegoers could always rely on quicksand to swallow Tarzan's enemies. But is there even a grain of truth in the killer quicksand story? Can you really be sucked down into a bottomless pit?

Me Tarzan— You in deep trouble!

Soil particles up close

Jamie up to his neck in quicksand

BUSTER SAYS:

The ground we step on is made up of individual particles of soil. If you examine a pile of dirt under a microscope, you'll see that each particle is in contact with a number of particles next to it. Each particle exerts a force on the ones touching it. This force, called friction, is what holds the particles together and gives the soil its strength. Quicksand is nothing more than a patch of land that has been oversaturated with water. When motion is added to these conditions, the water gets trapped in place. That's because there's not enough time for the water in the pores of the soil to seep out. When the soil particles lose contact with each other, the force or friction between the soil particles is lost and the soil loses the ability to support weight. Motion keeps these particles moving. The whole process is called liquefaction.

AIRHEADS:

Jamie and Adam inflate a pool to serve as a catch basin and water recycler for the quicksand box. A crane moves the tank into position in the pool's center. Before filling the pool, Adam and Jamie have a little blow-up of their own. Jamie wants to use a garden hose that will fill the pool in about five hours, while Adam is in favor of a more expensive but much speedier method—a fire hose that would get the job done in 15 or 20 minutes. The two finally settle on the more cost-effective garden hose.

Fire hose!

Garden hose!

PRESSING PROBLEMS:

Now for the sand—all 20,000 pounds of it. An engineering geologist confirms that the fine sand the MythBusters have selected is perfect for making quicksand. But before the water is pumped in, the gigantic bag of sand has to be moved into position above the tank. Adam has volunteered for the job. Behind the controls of a crane he expertly lifts the massive bag of sand above the tank. The bag drains, filling the tank.

BLAST FROM THE PAST

Earthquakes can produce something like quicksand in an instant. As the earth shifts, the ground swishes back and forth like water in a washing machine. As the water pressure increases, the ground turns to mush and gives way.

The year was 1964, the place Niigata, Japan. An earthquake with a magnitude of 7.5 hit the city. The ground quivered and shook, causing hundreds of buildings to tilt like castles in the sand. After the tremors stopped, the undamaged buildings were hoisted back into place.

STICK IN THE MUD:

Adam and Jamie are pumped. Their giant sandbox is about to be turned into quicksand. As a precaution, they've made sure that they have plenty of tools on hand: a vine, a walking stick, and a bar stretched across the tank to grab onto for a worst-case scenario.

#@$*%!

GO TIME:

The pump is switched on. Bummer! The holes Adam made were supposed to let out the water before it reached the top of the pile. But the sand is so fine it's clogging the holes. Adam and Jamie substitute cotton batting for the gauze, hoping the larger surface area will allow more water to flow through while still holding back the sand. Earlier, a member of the MythBusters' build team had made a hydrometer to tell how dense, or thick, the quicksand is compared to plain water. The quicksand turns out to be denser than water. That means in theory it should be easier to float in quicksand.

Cotton batting

IN THE MIX:

The pump is turned on again and water rises through the sand. This time it's working perfectly. When the mixture becomes quicksand, Adam climbs in. The quicksand reaches to his chest. Adam experiences a real sinking feeling. Will he be sucked under? When the pump is turned off, Adam is pleasantly surprised. He is far less dense than the quicksand, and he floats like a cork.

UP NEXT:

Jamie takes a turn. He floats with ease, too. Neither of them needs the vine, or any of the tools they have on hand in case of emergency.

CONCLUSION:

Is Hollywood-style killer quicksand real or a myth? It looks like Adam and Jamie have proven that this is one myth that has been completely busted. Although people and animals have been injured or even died from being immersed in quicksand, the reason is due either to exposure to the elements or because they can't escape, not because they are sucked under.

BUSTED!

DO TRY THIS AT HOME

Make your own version of quicksand by using cornstarch instead of sand. The cornstarch mixture will mimic the behavior of real quicksand.

Materials:

- Drop cloth for the floor
- One 16-oz. box of cornstarch
- Large mixing bowl
- Between 1 and 2 cups of water
- Mixing spoon
- Marble or other small object
- Large self-sealing plastic bag

1. Place a drop cloth under your work area to catch any spills.
2. Pour 4 ounces of the cornstarch ($\frac{1}{4}$ of the box) into a mixing bowl. Slowly add about $\frac{1}{2}$ cup of water and stir.
3. Alternate adding a small amount of cornstarch and a small amount of water to your mixture until it has the consistency of molasses or honey.
4. Stick your hand into the mixture. How does it feel? Move your hand around slowly. Now try to move it fast. What happened? If the "quicksand" is the right consistency, the faster you move your hand, the thicker and more like a solid it feels. Go to the bottom of the bowl and try to grab some "quicksand" and pull it to the surface. That's what it feels like to sink into real quicksand!
5. Drop a marble or some other small object into your mixture and then try to pull it out. Was this easy or hard to do?
6. When you're finished, seal up the mixture in a plastic bag and dispose of it in the garbage. Be sure not to throw the mixture down the sink as it will stop up the drain and clog pipes.

BUSTER SAYS:

Did you know that the mixture you just made is an exception to an important law of physics? Sir Isaac Newton, a scientist who lived from 1642—1727, figured out that all fluids have a measurable thickness known as viscosity. Liquids that flow easily, such as water, have a low viscosity. Liquids that are hard to pour, such as honey or ketchup, have a high viscosity. According to Newton's law of viscosity, changes in temperature cause changes in viscosity. When you heat honey, it becomes easier to pour. But the mixture of water and cornstarch you just made doesn't become easier to pour when it is heated. Unlike other liquids, its viscosity is actually increased by force of motion.

BRAINBUSTERS

Are you a quicksand expert? Take this true/false quiz and find out.

1. People can drown in quicksand because it acts like a vacuum cleaner sucking them below the surface.

2. Quicksand is a bottomless pit.

3. The reason you do not sink into dry sand is friction.

4. The best place to find quicksand is in the desert.

5. Viscosity is the measurement of how fast or slow a liquid can be poured.

6. Hot syrup is harder to pour than cold syrup.

7. Quicksand is always made of sand.

8. A good place to get an idea about how quicksand works is near a beach.

9. If you step into quicksand, the best thing to do is to move very slowly.

10. Friction causes buildings to sink during an earthquake.

Answers on page 141

ANSWERS TO BRAINBUSTER QUIZZES

CHAPTER 1

1. False: Galileo, a famous 16th-century scientist, discovered that objects fall to Earth at the same speed no matter what their weight.

2. False: The marble will land first because air will get in the way of the feather and hold it back. Wind resistance is friction, too.

3. False: Wax reduces the friction between the ski and snow, making the skier go faster.

4. True: Rough surfaces on the bottoms of footwear increase friction so they grip the ground better.

5. False: Gravity, not friction, is the force that keeps us firmly anchored to Earth.

6. True: Wheels make it possible to move heavy loads more efficiently because they reduce the friction between surfaces.

7. False: Heavier objects have more inertia, so it is easier to stop the empty barrel.

8. True: Objects at rest do not want to move and moving objects do not want to stop.

9. False: Although you overcome inertia to send the ball into the air, it's gravity that pulls the ball back down.

10. False: As the wave gets closer to the shore, friction from the sand slows it down at the bottom. However, the top of the wave continues at the same speed and falls over the bottom because of gravity.

CHAPTER 2

1. False: Plants need sunlight to grow and it's pretty dark inside your stomach. It's still not a good idea to swallow watermelon or other seeds. They can get lodged in your throat, and some, such as apple seeds and cherry pits, contain small amounts of cyanide, which could make you sick. But if you happen to swallow a watermelon seed don't worry about it. It will probably just pass right through your system and come out the other end.

2. False: While Americans often use these terms interchangeably, a true yam comes from a completely different plant family than the sweet potato. Yams, which originated in Africa, are grown in the Caribbean and are not widely available here. Sweet potatoes originated in South America and are grown in the United States. Most "yams" sold in supermarkets are a variety of sweet potato. Incidentally, neither the yam nor the sweet potato is closely related to the potato.

3. True: A study by Ohio State University and the American Society of Florists fed rats high doses of pulverized poinsettia leaves, which didn't harm them or cause any side effects. While it's still not a good idea to eat poinsettias—or any other houseplant, for that matter—the worst that could happen to you or your pet is an upset stomach.

4. True: The luak, or palm civet, is a small mammal native to Indonesia that has a particular fondness for the fruit of the coffee plant. The beans pass through its system undigested and are deposited in its droppings. This process leaves the beans slightly fermented, which apparently adds to the richness of the resulting coffee. While the task of collecting the beans may be rather unpleasant, the fact that they can fetch more than $100 per pound probably more than makes up for it.

5. True: Ricin, a poison found in the seeds of the castor bean plant, is 12 thousand times stronger than rattlesnake venom. It takes no more than two-millionths of an ounce to kill the average-sized adult.

6. False: Although hummingbirds do sip nectar from honeysuckle flowers, their humming sound is made by their flapping wings.

7. True: The plant was a durian, a tropical Asian plant with fruit so foul-smelling it has been banned in Indonesian subways and restaurants because its odor has caused nausea in people in its vicinity.

8. True: A tree nettle plant in Indonesia has branches coated with tiny hairs that contain strong toxins. The plant is so dangerous that animals and humans can die just from touching it!

9. True: Some plants need meat to survive. One such plant, the Nepthenses, which grows in the rainforests of Southeast Asia, consumes rats, frogs, and small birds that land on it.

10. False: A special strain of cotton developed by botanist C. L. Spears grows in a variety of colors.

CHAPTER 3

1. True: Goldfish have 96 chromosomes, while humans have only 46.

2. False: However, the owner of a carp named Falstaff reported it regularly stuck its head out of its pond to touch noses with Chino, a golden retriever.

3. True: Once a year, for the past 673 years, it's been the custom for the mayor of Grammot, Belgium, and the members of the city council to each drink a cup of wine containing a goldfish.

4. True: The young salmon swim in a tank that is set within a larger one filled with cod, their main predator. By watching how the cod try to attack them, the salmon learn the best ways to get away from them.

5. False: A parrot fish gets its name from its parrot-like mouth.

6. False: A mob is a group of kangaroos. A group of jellyfish is a smuck.

7. True: For the first two years of their lives, all sand crabs are male. Then, when they are two, they turn into females and start to lay eggs.

8. True: *Linckia columbiae* is a species of starfish that can grow back completely from a severed piece less than an inch long.

9. False: A male blanket octopus never grows larger than two-thirds of an inch. The females of the species have been known to exceed 6 feet in length.

10. False: After a phronima sedentaria shrimp deposits its eggs in a salp, a sea organism, it pushed the salp around like a baby carriage until the eggs have hatched.

CHAPTER 4

1. True: An octopus named Frieda learned how to twist open jars with her tentacles after watching her keepers at the Hellabrunn Zoo in Munich, Germany, open jars of her food each day. She'll only open jars that contain her very special treats though, ignoring those that contain ordinary fish.

2. True: Lazzaro Spallanzani performed a variety of experiments that proved that bits of food contained in vomit continue to be digested outside the stomach.

3. True: There are 35 million miniscule vats inside your stomach that produce acid. The acid breaks up food so that the nutrients can be absorbed by your body.

4. False: More bacteria live in your mouth than in any other place in your body. Over 100 million bacteria feast off the leftover food particles they find there.

5. False: This myth stems from the fact that for humans, a dog bite is less likely to get infected than a bite from another human. Many harmful bacteria are species-specific, so most of the bacteria in a dog's mouth are harmless to humans, but may cause an infection in another dog.

6. True: Oral bacteria can get into the bloodstream through a wound in the tongue and make its way to the heart, resulting in endocarditis, a serious inflammation of the heart valves or tissues. Additionally, oral piercings can cause a whole host of complications, including damage to the teeth and gums, bleeding, nerve damage, and interference with dental X-rays.

7. False: Curved little worms about a half-inch long, hookworms live in soil that has been contaminated by human feces. The worms make their way inside a human host by boring through the soles of bare feet.

8. False: Children are the primary hosts to pinworms. No thicker than a straight pin, these tiny, curly, white worms lay microscopic eggs that are so light they can float in the air. They're picked up on doorknobs and other surfaces in public places. When children touch their fingers to their mouths, they swallow the microscopic eggs, which then hatch in the intestine.

9. True: A long flat worm made up of segments, each of which is capable of producing thousands of eggs, the tapeworm uses the hooks and the sucker on its head to attach itself to the inside of the small intestine, where it feeds on digested food.

10. True: *Grossology* is a traveling interactive exhibit where children learn about the human body by interacting with the exhibits.

CHAPTER 5

1. False: Australian funnel web spiders are easy to milk because their fangs are so large.

2. True: The raft spider's favorite place to hang out is in the water. Sensitive to the slightest ripple, this hefty creature knows when a frog or fish is nearby. Once it spots its prey, it quickly stabs it with its fangs and carries it back to shore to eat it.

3. False: Most spiders eat other spiders. In fact, the bulk of a daddy longlegs' diet consists of other spiders.

4. False: The Brazilian wandering spider has enough venom stored in its glands to kill 250 mice.

5. True: The word *arachnid* is derived from Arachne, a Greek woman turned into a spider by the Goddess Athena for challenging the goddess's spinning ability.

6. False: Webs vary from species to species, but all spiders of the same species spin the same types of webs. Some scientists believe that the webs, which mimic the patterns reflected by flowers in ultraviolet light, are meant to attract insects. The insects confuse the webs with the flowers they're looking for.

7. False: Spiders use their fangs to inject their prey with a digestive juice that liquefies their insides so they can be easily sucked up.

8. False: The mother wolf spider carries her babies on her back until they are strong enough to fend for themselves.

9. False: Spiders produce a variety of silk that is tailor-made for each purpose. Some silk is for making drag lines to travel on; another type is for protecting eggs. Still another type is for wrapping up food to save for later.

10. True: Bolas spiders spin a silken thread that ends in a sticky substance. When the bolas spies a tasty morsel, it hurls the thread at its prey, trapping it with the sticky stuff, then reels in its dinner.

CHAPTER 6

1. False: Although Thomas Crapper, a plumber in England, obtained many patents for plumbing-related products, there is no evidence that he ever got one for inventing the flush toilet. In 1778, Alexander Cummings received the first patent for an early version of the toilet used today.

2. True: Because restrooms in ancient Greece featured multiple seating, it was possible for people to visit the bathroom and talk to their neighbors at the same time.

3. False: Due to gravity, astronauts use suction toilets to prevent their urine from floating around their space capsule in little bubbles. Like vacuum cleaners, toilets in space suck body waste into containers. Sometimes the urine is recycled into drinking water.

4. False: The human gut is full of good bacteria that help us digest our food.

5. True: When Maine's Sugarloaf ski resort was overrun with tourists, the town could not handle all the extra sewage. So they cleverly devised a way to make use of it. They had the sewage travel to a plant where it was treated with chemicals to cleanse it of harmful bacteria. It was then piped to another plant where it was frozen and then sprayed out through snow machines.

6. True: A Japanese scientist has designed a toilet capable of analyzing waste and sending that information electronically to doctors—information such as how much the users weigh and the amount of fat and sugar in their waste.

7. False: During Victorian times, chamber pots were often beautifully decorated. Some made political statements by displaying in the interiors likenesses of important figures of the time. Some played a tune as they were being used!

8. True: In 2001, Lam Sai-wing of Hong Kong created a toilet out of solid gold for a bathroom whose ceiling is covered with diamonds, rubies, sapphires, and emeralds.

9. False: Actually, London features a new line of state-of-the-art self-cleaning toilets that pop out of the ground at night when most other restrooms are closed. They are pulled back underground in the morning by remote control.

10. True: The Kohler Design Center in Wisconsin proudly displays a 30-foot tower of toilets. At the facility there is also a museum featuring toilets through the ages.

CHAPTER 7

1. False: You can't steer a hot-air balloon; it takes you where the wind blows.

2. True: The largest airship ever built, the *Hindenburg* was more than 800 feet long.

3. False: The *Hindenburg* was extremely luxurious. It even had a baby-grand piano in its lounge.

4. True: The passengers on the first hot-air balloon were all animals: a sheep, a duck, and a rooster.

5. False: On November 21, 1783, two French noblemen went on a 25-minutes flight launched by the Montgolfier brothers, Joseph and Ettienne. They started in Paris and landed in a vineyard 5 miles away.

6. False: The opposite is true. Hot air takes up more space than the same volume of cold air. That's why a balloon will pop if placed on a radiator.

7. False: Pilatre de Rozier was killed in his attempt to cross the English Channel, his craft exploding a half-hour after takeoff.

8. True: On January 9, 1793, George Washington witnessed the first hot-air balloon flight in North America. Jean-Pierre Blanchard manned the balloon in Philadelphia and landed in Gloucester County, New Jersey.

9. False: In 1988, Per Lindstrand set a record by reaching a height of 65,000 feet in his hot-air balloon.

10. False: Hot-air ballooning was out of fashion for a quite a long time. It's only in the last 50 years that the sport has gained in popularity.

CHAPTER 8

1. True: Transportation officials in New York City found themselves with a number of retired subway cars and no place to put them. The state of Delaware was searching for large metal objects to create artificial reefs. The solution to both problems was to sink the subway cars off the coast of Delaware and create artificial reefs. The reefs have since attracted a variety of fish to the area.

2. False: Divers who explore the *Titanic* are concerned because the ship is being consumed at the rate of 200 pounds per day by microbes called rusticules, not swordfish.

3. False: A hypothermal vent, an undersea volcano, is a harsh environment for animals to live in, but live they do. Despite the complete darkness, lack of oxygen, poisonous gases, and extremes of temperature and pressure found there, tubeworms and a few other hardy creatures thrive in this inhospitable place.

4. False: Because the *Andrea Doria* lies relatively close to sea level, more divers have visited it than any other shipwreck.

5. True: In the late 1600s, the ship *La Belle* sank off the coast of Texas. When it was discovered in 1986, explorers found the skeleton of its captain, the French explorer Renee La Salle, tucked inside a coil of rope. The brain within the 300-year-old skull was perfectly preserved.

6. True: A ship sailed about 5 miles from the place where the *Titanic* went down. Its captain saw the flares but mistook them for fireworks.

7. True: Another word for rust is *oxidation*. In order to rust, metal has to be exposed to oxygen. Since the Black Sea is devoid of oxygen, explorers have found that ships that sink there never rust.

8. False: Marine archaeologists' prime obstacles are curious octopuses that move objects before they can be catalogued.

9. False: The deepest parts of the ocean are called the trenches. They can dip to 35,640 feet below sea level.

10. False: Deep-sea divers wear protective gear to protect them from the crushing force of water pressure.

CHAPTER 9

1. False: Rainbows are produced when the sun breaks out from behind clouds while it is raining. As sunlight travels through the raindrops, it is bent, splitting the sunlight into the colors in a rainbow—red, orange, yellow, green, blue, indigo, and violet.

2. False: Rain clouds are so thick that they block light from the sun. If you fly above the clouds in an airplane, you'll notice that the tops are white.

3. True: It rains for 350 days a year in Mount Wai-ale-ale, Hawaii.

4. True: Acid rain forms when nitrogen and other chemicals in car and truck exhaust fumes unite with moisture in the air. Acid rain has caused more damage to the Parthenon, an ancient Greek temple, than 2,000 years of wind and rain.

5. True: Such a well is called an artesian well, a man-made well drilled deep into the earth where water is trapped in a layer of very porous rock like sandstone. The sandstone lies between thick layers of rock above and below it. Because the water is so deep, it is usually pure and free from pollutants.

6. True: The winds inside cumulonimbus clouds can reach a speed of 124 miles per hour, about as fast as most express trains.

7. False: Stratus clouds spread across the sky in a horizontal pattern, while cumulonimbus clouds can be 11 miles tall, which is twice as tall as Mt. Everest.

8. False: Though Seattle, Washington, gets more than its share of rain, the world record for the most rain in one minute was set on July 4, 1956 at Unionville, Maryland, with a downpour of 1.23 inches.

9. False: A drop of water may travel thousands of miles between the time it evaporates into the atmosphere and the time it falls as rain.

10. False: Most of the water droplets in a cloud evaporate. Just one-fifth eventually falls as rain.

CHAPTER 10

1. False: Sound travels four times faster through water than through air. It can travel such long distances that whales can hear each other from approximately 100 miles away.

2. False: As a vacuum, space is soundless. Sound needs to travel through a media, such as air or water.

3. False: Concert-stage designers aim to use echoes well, not eliminate them, in order to create the best possible sound.

4. True: Sound waves usually travel in concentric circles, like ripples made by a stone thrown into water. A perfectly curved stage reflects sound waves in a straight line so that they reach everyone in the room at about the same time.

5. True: It's easier for a sound wave to bounce off a hard surface than a soft one. That's why you don't hear echoes in rooms with fabric-covered walls.

6. False: Light travels faster than sound, so you see a flash of lightning before you hear the sound waves of thunder.

7. True: Because sound waves travel well in water, scientists can make sound waves on the ocean floor with a special instrument called an oscillator. Then they use a fathometer to measure the amount of time it takes for the sound waves to bounce back. This allows them to estimate the water's depth.

8. False: Blowing on a bottle makes a sound because the air in the bottle vibrates.

9. False: On a computer screen, high-frequency sounds appear as waves that are close together. Low-frequency sounds are far apart.

10. True: The bottle with more water has less air to vibrate, which is why the sound produced by blowing on it is higher than the bottle with less water and more air.

CHAPTER 11

1. True: Weightlessness causes objects to become lighter in space, where they are far away from the gravitational pull of the planets.

2. False: Every day Earth's atmosphere is penetrated by 75,000,000 meteors.

3. True: When large stars die, they explode and then become extremely heavy and compact.

4. False: Space shuttles land like gliders and don't use fuel at all.

5. True: Isaac Newton, a scientific genius, discovered these laws in 1687.

6. True: Valentina Tereshkova was a factory worker in the former Soviet Union who was chosen for space training when she took up parachuting as a hobby.

7. False: Before entering his spacecraft, Gagarin ate a breakfast of chopped meat, blackberry jam, and coffee.

8. False: The largest meteorite that ever fell to Earth left a hole 112 miles wide.

9. False: Because Pluto is so small and its gravity weak, you would weight one-third of your weight on Earth.

10. False: Every second the sun gives off enough energy to fill the energy needs of the United States for 50 million years.

CHAPTER 12

1. False: A megabyte is a unit of computer memory. A hertz is a unit of frequency.

2. True: If you hold a note of the same frequency long enough, resonance will build in the glass until it shatters.

3. True: When the vibrations of an earthquake equal the natural frequency of a building, resonance causes the building to shake so hard that it collapses. The building left standing may have had a different natural frequency.

4. False: When tapped, two identical glasses filled with the same amount of water will sound the same because they will vibrate at the same frequency.

5. False: The pendulum of a grandfather clock makes it keep the correct time. The pendulum's natural frequency makes it swing at the same pace, which keeps the clock ticking with regularity.

6. False: The shorter pendulum will swing faster because it has a higher frequency.

7. False: The collapse of a bridge during an earthquake demonstrates resonance, a phenomenon that occurs when the frequency of the earth's vibration matches the natural frequency of the bridge. The vibration grows in strength or amplitude until the bridge collapses.

8. False: Tightening the string of an instrument increases the frequency of the vibration which in turn increases its pitch.

9. True: The natural frequencies of the two bells are so similar to one another that a sympathetic vibration or resonance is created between the two.

10. False: To achieve maximum amplitude or height on a swing, you have to time your pumps to occur just as the swing is changing direction.

CHAPTER 13

1. False: Light travels at different speeds depending on the substance it's traveling through. For instance, light travels faster through air than through water or glass.

2. False: A smooth, shiny surface reflects more light than a rough, dark one. That's why joggers are advised to wear white clothing at night and cyclists should have shiny reflectors on their bicycles.

3. False: The Earth is closer to the sun in January, and farthest from the sun in July. In the summer, even though we're slightly farther from the sun, the Northern Hemisphere is tilted so the sun's rays hit it more directly than they do in the wintertime.

4. True: You should never look directly at the sun, even while wearing dark glasses, because direct sunlight can damage your retina, the light-sensitive nerve endings in the back of the eye, causing impaired vision or blindness.

5. True: While most car windshields and newer windows in homes are treated to filter out the sun's UV rays, they can't block them entirely, so it's possible to get burned through a window.

6. False: Concave mirrors make objects look larger than they would in a flat mirror.

7. True: Convex mirrors make objects look smaller than those reflected in a flat mirror. They're attached to cars because they gather light from a wide area, giving drivers a good view of what's going on behind them.

8. False: Funhouse mirrors are made up of both convex and concave mirrors, giving the images they reflect a strange, distorted look.

9. True: On a very hot day, you might see what looks like a pool of water on a road that is completely dry. This happens because hot air is bending the suns rays, creating a mirage that makes the road look wet when it's not.

10. True: Place a straw in a glass half-filled with water. Although the straw is straight, it will appear to be bent because light rays change direction when they enter the water.

CHAPTER 14

1. False: The saltwater is the electrolyte. In the Baghdad battery, it's the lemon juice.

2. True: Static electricity is what makes hair stand on end. A comb or brush rubs electrons off each strand of hair, causing them to become electrically charged. Because the strands of hair have the same charge, they repel each other.

3. True: Friction from your shoes rubs electrons off the carpet and they build up in your body. When you touch something metal, like the doorknob, the extra electrons jump to the metal creating a little spark. Clouds in a thunderstorm also rub against each other, accumulating large amounts of electrons that create a big spark called lightning.

4. True: Luigi Galvani (1737–1798), an Italian scientist, caused contractions to occur in a frog's legs by touching its nerves with a charged piece of metal. Not fully understanding how electricity worked, this early scientist believed he had discovered a new kind of electricity. He called it "animal electricity."

5. False: Batteries "die" when they run out of electrolyte, or battery acid.

6. True: An automobile frame is attached to a giant battery, turning it into an electrode. Then it's dipped into a zinc solution and the zinc is evenly plated onto the bottom of the metal frame. This is modern rust-proofing.

7. False: The nucleus is the center of an atom, the building block from which all matter is made. Electrons are charged particles that orbit the nucleus.

8. False: An electric current is tiny charged particles called electrons moving through metal wire from one side of a battery to the other.

9. False: Nails and screws are electroplated with zinc to keep them from rusting.

10. False: Galvanization, named after Luigi Galvani, is the process for rust-proofing.

CHAPTER 15

1. False: If you step into quicksand, it will not suck you down. Your own movements will cause you to dig yourself deeper into it. Quicksand is more buoyant than water so it's easier to float in it than in a swimming pool.

2. False: Most quicksand is usually no more than a few feet deep.

3. True: Friction is the force that gives soil its strength, allowing it to support weight. Moisture and motion disrupt that force.

4. False: Desert sand lacks the key ingredient that quicksand needs, which is water. Quicksand usually forms above a bubbling spring near a body of water, such as a lake, river, or ocean.

5. True: All fluids have a property known as viscosity. Liquids that are easy to pour have low viscosity, while liquids that are hard to pour have high viscosity.

6. False: According to Newton's law of viscosity, when you heat a liquid with high viscosity, it will lose some of its viscosity.

7. False: Quicksand can be made of clay or silt. In fact, under the right conditions, any fine-grained soil can turn into quicksand.

8. True: When you walk on dry sand far from the shore, the sand supports your weight just fine. Walk closer to the water's edge though, and you'll find that your feet leave deep footprints where they've sunk into the sand. That's because the oversaturated sand combined with the motion of the waves have caused the top layers to lose their strength.

9. True: If you thrash around in quicksand, it becomes more difficult to move. That's because the force of motion increases quicksand's viscosity.

10. False: Liquefaction is the property that causes the ground to give way during earthquakes.

GLOSSARY

acid   a sour-tasting substance that joins with an alkali to form a salt.

alkali   a strong base that joins with an acid to form a salt.

anechoic chamber   a sound-absorbent room that does not produce echoes.

arachnid   a class of eight-legged animals that includes spiders, scorpions, and ticks.

arachnophobia   fear of spiders.

atom   the tiniest particle of an element.

bacteria   microscopic one-celled organisms, many of which cause disease.

battery   a chemical source of electricity.

chlorophyll   a green pigment found in plants' leaves that lets plants perform photosynthesis.

circuit   a loop of electrical conductors that allows current to flow in an unbroken ring from the energy source and back.

conductor   a material that carries electricity.

density   the mass of a substance for a given volume.

echo   reflected sound.

electricity   a form of energy carried by particles that are negatively and positively charged.

electrolyte   the material that allows electricity to flow between positive and negative electrodes.

electron   a negatively charged particle that circles an atom's nucleus.

electroplating   the coating of one metal with the thin layer of another.

frequency   the number of vibrations per second, measured in hertz.

friction   the force that resists movement when one surface rubs against another.

gravity   the force that pulls matter to the center of the Earth.

helium   a colorless, odorless, inert gas, the second lightest of all the elements.

hydrogen   a colorless, odorless, highly flammable gas, the lightest of all the elements.

liquefaction   the change of a solid or gas to a liquid.

molecule   the smallest particle of a substance that has all its chemical properties.

photosynthesis   a process in which green plants turn the sun's energy into food.

pitch   the highness or lowness of a sound's vibrations.

quicksand   loose sand mixed with water which yields to pressure.

resonance   a vibration produced in reaction to another vibration.

sound waves   vibrations in the air, in a solid, or in a liquid, that cause us to perceive sound.

terminal velocity   the maximum velocity, or speed, that a falling object can achieve.

thrust   the force propelling an airplane or rocket.

trireme   a Roman warship with three sets of oars.

venom   a poison secreted by certain animals, such as snakes and spiders.

WHERE TO FIND OUT MORE

WEBSITES

Check out these web sites to learn more about the science and history behind the MythBusters shows. Many of these sites include fun quizzes and activities for you to try.

NASA Kids: Rockets
http://kids.msfc.nasa.gov/rockets
Discover the rockets behind NASA's space program.

Biology of Plants
http://mbgnet.mobot.org/bioplants/main.html
An overview of all things green; includes an easy-to-understand explanation of photosynthesis.

Test Your Pet
http://www.bbc.co.uk/sn/tvradio/programmes/testyourpet
Whatever type of pet you have—a dog, a cat, a rabbit, or a goldfish—you can test its IQ by following the instructions on this site.

Stomach Gurgles
http://yucky.kids.discovery.com/noflash/body/yuckystuff/gurgle
Listen to what it sounds like when a stomach digests food.

The Spider Myths Site
http://www.washington.edu/burkemuseum/spidermyth
Check out this site to learn the true story behind popular spider myths.

Stalking the Mysterious Microbe
http://www.microbe.org
Learn cool facts and trivia about bacteria and other microbes.

Buoyancy Brainteasers
http://www.pbs.org/wgbh/nova/lasalle/buoyancy.html
Test your knowledge of why things sink or float with these puzzlers.

Web Weather for Kids
http://eo.ucar.edu/webweather
Besides performing cool activities, learn how to forecast the weather.

Science of Sound
http://www.sci.mus.mm.us/sound
Explore the world of sound.

The Science of Light
http://www.learner.org/teacherslab/science/light
Learn more about light and color on this site.

Super Bridge
http://www.pbs.org/wgbh/nova/bridge/meetsusp.html
Find out more about suspension bridges and view the collapse of the Tacoma Narrows Bridge on this PBS site.

Friction
http://www.sci.mus.mn.us/sln/tf/f/friction/friction.html
Check out a fun experiment with friction.

IEEE Virtual Museum
http://www.ieee.com/museum
Get turned on to the wonders of electricity.

How Stuff Works
http://science.howstuffworks.com/quicksand.htm
Discover how quicksand works and how to safely escape from its grasp.

INDEX

PHOTO CREDITS

With the following exceptions, all photographic images in this book are courtesy of Discovery Communications, Inc.:
p. 8 Kirsten Hall; pp. 16 (peas), 24, 48 (toilet and toothbrush), 51 (toothbrush), 56, 64, 74, 100 (bridge) AbleStock;
p. 32 Brian Skerry/National Geographic; pp. 40, 118 Atif Toor; p. 71 North Wind Picture Archives; p. 128 Photofest.